# YOU'VE DONE WHAT, MY LORD?

Rumshott is one of the finest landed estates in England. However, when James Aden takes up the position of Deputy Agent he does not realise the full extent of what the job entails. He finds himself spending his days negotiating with royalty, farmers, and even wildlife, as well as the imperious Lady Leghorn. In order to survive, James must come to terms with his role quickly, and not let himself get too distracted by Sophie, the pre-college assistant.

# YOU'VE DONE WHAT, MY LORD?

*by*

Rory Clark

**Magna Large Print Books**
Long Preston, North Yorkshire,
BD23 4ND, England.

British Library Cataloguing in Publication Data.

Clark, Rory
    You've done what, my lord?

    A catalogue record of this book is
    available from the British Library

    ISBN    978-0-7505-3840-4

First published in the UK by Robinson,
an imprint of Constable & Robinson Ltd., 2013

Cover illustration © Joe Roberts by arrangement with
Constable & Robinson Ltd.

Published in Large Print 2013 by arrangement with
Constable & Robinson Ltd.

Magna Large Print is an imprint of Library Magna Books Ltd.

Printed and bound in Great Britain by
T.J. (International) Ltd., Cornwall, PL28 8RW

To my mother and father with love

# Acknowledgements

My sincere thanks to Hal Norman for his editorial guidance and enthusiasm without which this book would still be on my desk.

# Chapter 1

I only got the job because of my shoes. Considering the job was managing 13,500 acres of prime English countryside for Henry, the Tenth Earl Leghorn, this was remarkable, although as time progressed I realised it was nothing out of the ordinary for the Leghorn family.

Rumshott Park had been the Leghorn seat for five hundred years. The family lived in the magnificent mansion house, isolated from the rest of the world by the rolling expanse of parkland within the estate's walled boundary. The house was the hub of the estate, the power centre, which controlled several square miles of countryside encompassing farms, woodland and villages.

The agent, whose job was to administer and coordinate the many different facets which made up the estate, was a forceful, determined man called George Pratt who had, I discovered, an obsession with shoes.

I had been working as a junior assistant agent for a duke in the West Country when I spotted an advertisement for a vacancy as deputy agent at Rumshott in Russetshire. Wanting to climb my way up the professional ladder I sent off an application. A few weeks passed by and I had rather put it out of my mind when one evening I received a telephone call.

'Hello, is that James Aden?' the voice boomed

at me down the line, daring me to be otherwise.

'Yes, speaking' I replied, not having a clue who should be shouting at me.

'George Pratt here at Rumshott, thanking you for your letter. I'd like to meet you. Can we sort something out for next week?' he commanded.

'Oh, um,' I responded rather lamely. 'That's very kind of you ... yes, I'm sure we could arrange a day. When were you thinking of?'

'Wednesday, ten o'clock, here at the estate office.'

'Right.' He seemed very blunt and businesslike. 'I'll check that I can take the day off and confirm it with you tomorrow if that's okay.'

'Excellent.' I winced as a high number of decibels penetrated my eardrum. I removed the handset from such close proximity in preparation for the next assault. 'Loved your letter and think you might be just the sort of chap we want here. Right experience. I do hope you'll be able to come over on Wednesday.' The enthusiasm could be heard echoing around the walls of my small sitting room.

I had not had time to consider the significance of the conversation before a thunderous goodbye ricocheted from the fireplace and the line went dead.

As peace returned to the West Country, the importance of this brief but loud exchange sank in. It appeared that I might have a very real chance of becoming the deputy agent at Rumshott – a prestigious and demanding position on one of the most sizeable and famous landed estates in the country.

The following Wednesday I was up at dawn in a state of nervous excitement. With great deliberation I chose my interview outfit. Deciding that I should wear the traditional land agent's uniform I pulled on some baggy fawn corduroy trousers, a well-cut tweed hacking jacket and, as luck would have it, a brand-new pair of Church's brogues, which I hadn't yet had occasion to wear.

I arrived early at Rumshott in time to have a short drive around the estate and a last-minute nervous pee in a hedge. After announcing my arrival at the estate office, I was kept waiting a few minutes. Sitting in the hall, trying to assume an air of confident nonchalance, I could hear a lot of crashing about and some indecipherable expletives from behind a closed door. I was beginning to wonder what on earth was going on when the door burst open, its hinges somehow remaining fixed to the frame, and a man launched himself into the middle of the reception hall.

'Morning, James Aden,' he shouted at me from a distance of eighteen inches, 'how kind of you to come and meet me.' He smiled warmly and shook my hand with a vice-like grip before leading me into his office.

George Pratt was very much as I had expected. He was a tall good-looking man in his early forties with lively piercing blue eyes and a strong smile. He had a slightly manic air about him, as though he believed there wasn't enough time in the day. His office bore this out. A large room adorned with some splendid oil paintings and substantial pieces of late eighteenth-century furniture, it was in complete disarray with files,

11

plans and papers everywhere. The crashing around that I'd heard earlier had obviously been the result of his efforts to find me a place to sit. The best he could do was a rather uncomfortable little wooden chair wedged between a marble bust of a long-deceased Leghorn and a grandfather clock that leant perilously towards me. Treading carefully, I negotiated the piles of paper stacked on the floor and was making remarkably good progress towards my allotted seat when Pratt shouted, 'Stop! Just look at that bloody thing there!'

Hovering delicately between a pile of pink files and a theodolite, I gave my impression of a startled hen, my head turning from side to side as I searched in vain for the object of his wrath.

'That file, that file by your right foot,' he bellowed, 'some damn woman has planted a bloody Leylandii hedge in her garden, which is completely against the rules on the estate.'

Not knowing how to respond I decided my best option was to make a last-minute dash for the relative safety of the chair.

'I won't have any of those dreadful suburban hedges on the estate,' he explained, 'and that file is full of the legal papers to get it removed.'

I had barely met the man but already I could sense that the rumours I had heard about Rumshott were true. I had been led to believe that it was not an easy place to work, that George Pratt's management was strict and that the fear and control exerted by Countess Leghorn was extraordinary. It was rapidly becoming clear the job would be no easy ride.

Mr Pratt settled down a little as he began to explain the make up of the estate – 8,500 acres at Rumshott, 2,500 in Norfolk, the same again in Gloucestershire, and property in London. In addition there was a glorious art collection and priceless furniture and china within the house. He explained about the staff and the various departments – the farm staff, forestry staff, gamekeepers, house and garden staff, those that worked in the office and the building maintenance team. All together there were about fifty full-time employees under his control.

'We'll just have a cup of coffee,' he offered, 'and I'll tell you about the family here.' Picking up the phone he barked at some unfortunate secretary that he wanted a pot of coffee brought through. I suspected that she could have heard him without the aid of the telephone.

'Lord Leghorn is the tenth earl and owns most of the Russetshire estate personally,' he began. 'The other estates are held in family trusts and we report to the trustees on matters concerning those. You probably know that Lord Leghorn suffered a serious stroke a few years ago. Although he's now in very good health his wife still has considerable influence on what we do here,' he explained. 'She has an extremely strong personality and it would be wrong of me to suggest that working for her is easy. She has determined views on what should happen and although she doesn't tend to involve herself directly in estate matters, her actions here in the house and park have repercussions elsewhere.'

There was a knock on the door and a well-dressed woman entered carrying a tray of coffee and biscuits.

'Here you are, Mr Pratt,' she said.

'Ah, Louise,' he bellowed. 'Thank you. Meet James Aden, who I'm interviewing for the job here.'

She teetered through the mounds of paper on some fashionable high-heeled shoes and balanced the tray on a pile of files occupying a corner of Pratt's vast leather-topped mahogany desk.

'Pleased to meet you,' she said, shaking my outstretched hand before teetering out again. She paused by the door.

'Mr Pratt, her ladyship phoned to make sure you hadn't forgotten to pay Partridges' bill. It must be paid today she said.'

'Right Lou, thank you,' he boomed as she closed the door.

'Now where was I? Ah, yes,' he started again. 'Lady Leghorn. Well you'd soon find out what she's like. Bark's worse than her bite. Then of course there's Lord Leghorn's four children – three girls and a boy. The son and heir is Lord Edward Rumshott who holds the courtesy title of Viscount Rumshott. He's unmarried and lives partly here and partly in London. All three girls are married: Lady Kate to a chap called Mortimer, chief umbrella holder to the Queen; Lady Caroline to a farmer called Juniper; and of course Lady Davina, now the Princess of Arnhustein.' As he paused to take a sip of coffee I noticed that he spent several seconds peering at my shoes.

'Davina's marriage has brought the family and estate into the public eye and the Leghorns are very sensitive to press intrusion. This is a bit of a problem for us here. Lady Leghorn and Viscount Rumshott are the most sensitive so we have to do our best and avoid any publicity, good or bad.'

He was staring at my shoes again, making me feel a little uncomfortable. I wondered if by some awful mishap I had trodden in some dog mess that was, as we were speaking, slowly slipping off the sole of my shoe and about to deposit itself on one of Pratt's scattered files. Surreptitiously I inspected the shoes' underside and, as the interview progressed, it seemed as though both the interviewer and the interviewee were intent merely on examining a pair of shoes.

However, there was no atrocity apparent on the soles of my brogues nor was there any pungent odour coming from them. I contented myself with the assumption that perhaps Mr Pratt was looking at his reflection in the highly polished toecaps.

'Both the countess and viscount get terribly jumpy if the press get hold of anything,' he continued, looking now at me, his attention drawn from my footwear. 'So it's vital that anyone doing this job is prepared to act with the utmost discretion,' he added sternly.

He glanced again briefly at my shoes before announcing that we ought to have a quick tour around some of the estate before lunch. By the time I had circumnavigated the unorthodox filing arrangement strewn across the carpet, Pratt was already in the hall yelling instructions to Louise.

'Right, we'll have a brief look at the house first

as the Leghorns are in London and then I'll show you a bit of the park.'

He leapt out of the estate office and practically ran across the wide expanse of carefully tended lawn crossing the south front of Rumshott House. It was difficult to take much in. We were accompanied initially by a housekeeper but she was soon left some way behind as Pratt raced through rooms of such grandeur that hours would have been needed to absorb their beauty and style properly. At speed they all blurred into a kaleidoscope of brilliant colours and grandiose schemes so that when we emerged from the house I had only the briefest idea of what the place was really like.

We walked back over the lawn towards the impressive sandstone stable block, which contained the estate office, whereupon I was hustled into the passenger seat of a large green Mercedes. Mr Pratt, it transpired, drove in the same manner in which he did everything else. Great concentration, speed and determination until some object of interest caught his eye and the intensity was redirected, causing the car to occasionally, if briefly, leave the road and wander slightly into the surrounding countryside.

I settled somewhat apprehensively into the deep leather seat and tried to absorb some of the serene beauty of our surroundings whilst listening to Mr Pratt's barrage of comments. The parkland around the house was beautifully kept, with cattle and sheep grazing content beneath the massive ancient oak trees that graced the rolling green acres. A lake mostly hidden by a fringe of woodland shimmered in the distance and as we approached the lodge gates I glimpsed a herd of deer standing motionless in a copse.

The road took us towards Great Bassett, the estate village of thatched roofs and roses clambering over walls set high in the gentle hills of Russetshire. The centuries-old church of St Peter and the street of ancient cottages were built in the local honey-coloured sandstone, while in the centre of a small green, outside a pub, stood an immense horse chestnut tree under which a couple of elderly parishioners sat on a bench enjoying the peaceful sunshine.

The powerful Mercedes cut a swathe through the bucolic reverie and we stopped abruptly in the car park of the Dog and Rabbit.

'We'll have a bite of lunch here,' shouted Pratt as he leapt from the car, 'and then I'll let you get on your way home.'

Inevitably he caused a commotion as he entered the pub. The low ceilings and heavy oak beams, which were silently sheltering a group of locals playing dominoes by the fireplace, suddenly reverberated with his cries of greetings to those he recognised. Most people seemed to know him and as the pub belonged to the estate he was treated with the type of deference and respect associated with a bygone era.

We sat down at a table by the window overlooking the village street and I tucked my well-polished shoes out of sight. I still hadn't fathomed what was wrong with them and, as Pratt was starting to question me about my experience and knowledge of the land agency profession, I didn't want the distraction of another foot inspection.

I was briefly disconcerted, however, by the unexpected voice of Buddy Holly blaring from the distant depths of the bar. Even Pratt found it difficult to compete.

'Can you turn that bloody thing off, Claude?' he bellowed at the publican. 'I can't hear myself think let alone talk.'

'Yes, Mr Pratt, sorry 'bout that. I'll turn 'im orf right away, Mr Pratt. Right away, sir.' Claude fumbled for the switch and there was a sudden silence punctuated only by the rapid crunching sound of Mr Pratt devouring a celery stick.

After lunch I was propelled at speed through a number of pretty stone villages, along winding country lanes with verges covered in clouds of white cow parsley. I was surprised at the beauty of this corner of Russetshire.

We drew up in a scattering of gravel outside the estate office, whereupon Mr Pratt said that he had to rush off to another appointment but that he would be in touch soon. As I reached to shake his hand and thank him for showing me around he had a final glance at my shoes and barked with an air of finality,

'Those are Church's brogues, aren't they?'

'Er, yes, they are,' I confirmed.

'Finest shoes in the world, you know. Absolute quality – no doubt about it. I always judge a man by his shoes. Never fails.'

And with that he disappeared with a roar of the engine, leaving me standing in the courtyard, my shoes coated in a layer of settling Russetshire dust.

# Chapter 2

After my first interview, George Pratt had liked me enough to recommend my appointment to Earl Leghorn. A meeting was hastily arranged to give his lordship the opportunity to assess me before a final decision was made. I arrived early and was exceedingly nervous about meeting a man I had often seen on television as the Princess of Arnhustein's father. I think Mr Pratt was a little nervous about it as well although he obviously thought I would fit in at the office. But my future depended on how I conducted myself in my interview with Lord Leghorn.

Once again I had gone to great lengths to dress appropriately and wore a clean pressed dark suit, my only handmade Jermyn Street shirt, a silk tie and my heavily polished shoes. I felt relatively composed, my mind was alert as the adrenalin raced around my body. I had swotted up on agricultural law and felt ready to answer any complicated legal questions the earl might throw at me – always a favourite at interviews. Mr Pratt chatted away as we walked over to the house but as we reached it my nerves started failing. The grandeur of the place and the prospect of an imminent meeting with an earl was overwhelming. I imagined that we would be shown into a library or formal drawing room by a liveried butler where the earl would be seated, impeccably attired, at a massive antique desk surrounded by ancestral portraits hung in their heavy gilt frames.

What happened was somewhat different. Mr Pratt showed me through into the private wing, which seemed unnaturally quiet. There did not seem to be any staff about so we continued on to his lordship's study. Mr Pratt knocked on the door. No answer. He peered in. No one there.

'Well I can't think where Lord Leghorn could be,' he said, surprised, 'it's 11.30 am, isn't it?'

'Um, yes, it is,' I replied. We walked back along the passage towards the main part of the house and met the housekeeper coming down the stairs.

'Morning, Jocelyn.'

'Good morning, Mr Pratt.'

'Do you know where his lordship is? I've got a meeting at 11.30 with him.'

'Oh,' she said sounding surprised, 'he's still in bed.'

'Still in bed,' he repeated incredulously. 'What the bloody hell's he doing in bed at this time of day? He's not ill, is he?'

'No, no. He just hasn't got up yet.'

'Good God above. He's supposed to be interviewing James Aden here. He can't have bloody well forgotten, surely!'

'Well he must have. I know he isn't expecting you. Could you come back later, or another day perhaps?'

Pratt was livid. 'No, we can't,' he barked at the unfortunate Jocelyn.

'Please go and tell his lordship that we're here and that James Aden is waiting for him having driven halfway across England to meet him.'

The firmness in his voice compelled Jocelyn to return upstairs and confront his lordship.

After an age she reappeared and asked us to wait in the study as his lordship was on his way. By now my expectations of the interview had altered and having got the earl out of bed I didn't suppose he would take kindly to me at all. I was lost in my negative thoughts waiting for the Right Honourable the Tenth Earl Leghorn, close friend of the Arnhustein Royal Family, father of Her Royal Highness the Princess of Arnhustein and grandfather of the future King of Arnhustein to stride into the room, when an unshaven tousle-haired chap came bumbling through the door wearing pyjamas and a tatty old pair of carpet slippers. Pratt stood up and with a start I realised it was the earl.

'G-good morning, good morning,' he said, slightly flustered. 'I-I'm s-sorry to have kept you waiting.'

'Good morning, my lord,' replied George, seemingly oblivious to his lordship's unusual interview attire. 'Can I introduce you to James Aden and then leave you to have a chat.'

'Morning. How d'you do?' His lordship smiled. 'Come and sit down,' he added, leading the way to some comfortable armchairs on the far side of the room.

I felt most incongruous and suddenly rather overdressed. I liked Lord Leghorn immediately and he soon put me at ease with his relaxed chatter and good humour. My revision had been wasted because we did not discuss a single point of land agency throughout the whole interview.

Altogether it was a rather strange experience and I doubt many people have ever been offered a job by a pyjama-clad earl.

I arrived at Rumshott a month later to take up my new job. I made an inauspicious start. During the first week, George asked me to travel with him to the Leghorn estate in Norfolk, Weston Ferretts. Following his instructions, I collected him from his house at six o'clock one morning in the smart new Golf GTI that I had been given with the job. It was, he said, a chance to give it a try on a long journey and I was looking forward to speeding up to the north Norfolk coast in it. Before falling asleep, George told me that we were to be in the Market Square at Downham Market by nine o'clock to meet an architect at his office. Confident that that was what he had said I left him to grunt and snore contentedly in the passenger seat.

Having only started at Rumshott the previous week I was a little nervous and still found the place and the people, particularly George, over-whelming. Relieved to draw up in the Market Square in Downham Market at ten minutes to nine with my boss still grunting like a contented sow, I pulled over to the kerb and leant into the back seat to find the file with the architect's address. It was then that he woke up with a yawn and a belch, peered hazily out of the window and asked why we had stopped.

'Well, we're here,' I explained.

He looked around.

'Where?'

'In the Market Square.'

'What bloody Market Square?'

'Downham Market, Market Square,' I continued, perplexed.

'Downham Market,' he repeated with incredulity. 'What the hell are we doing in Downham Market?'

'We're meeting the architect at nine o'clock.'

'In Burnham Market!'

'What? You said Downham Market when we left.'

'I did not,' he retorted. 'Why the hell would we come here?'

'Well I don't know,' I replied, convinced that he had said Downham Market. I didn't know Norfolk, I'd never been to Norfolk in my life. This was horribly embarrassing.

'Well we're in a right mess now, aren't we? Bang on nine o'clock in the wrong town on the wrong side of Norfolk.'

Unfortunately the day progressed badly as we were then late for every scheduled meeting. To make matters worse, George did not seem to want to sleep on the way home, preferring to mutter something about navigation and map reading.


## Chapter 3

Despite my early setback, a few months later I had managed to establish myself as the deputy agent and George was able to take a back seat, resolved only to get involved with major policy issues while day-to-day management was left up to me. My role as deputy agent on a large rural estate was an interesting and rewarding one but made that much more challenging by the added dynamics of Lady Leghorn's input.

She was predictably unpredictable and although we got on well enough, every now and then she would exert her influence, usually when some calamity had occurred. Theoretically her ladyship had no involvement with the estate, after all it was a 'country thing' as she put it, all muddy, smelly with horrible wild animals running around and definitely not her preferred environment. She kept her management skills focused on opening the house to the public and looking after the tourism side. Thirty thousand visitors a year would wander through the house and then visit her ladyship's tea room and gift shop, which were located uncomfortably close to the estate office in the stable block.

Her ladyship had, as one would expect, a separate house opening account in which all her receipts were deposited and expenses met. However, she managed the account with an alarming philosophy and whenever she found she was short of money she would march into the office and demand some more from the estate account. It made budgeting an uncertain science.

One morning in early summer I was sitting at my desk in what had been George's old office with the sun streaming into the courtyard from a Mediterranean-blue sky when I heard her ladyship arrive in the reception hall. The sky seemed to cloud over instantly as she said to Louise,

24

'NO, THAT WON'T DO AT ALL. I want to speak to George NOW.'

'I'm sorry my lady but he's in a meeting,' Louise replied.

'I DON'T CARE. He'll speak to me. Buzz him on that phone or whatever you do. Go on, do what I tell you.'

I could hear this going on through my closed door and was sorely tempted to pretend I hadn't. A scene that I did not want to get involved in was about to take place but my conscience got the better of me and I went through into the hall to help Louise.

'Good morning, Lady Leghorn,' I said.

She turned and beamed an exuberant smile, the proverbial siren drawing the ships on to the rocks.

'Can I help you?'

'No,' she replied, 'I need George urgently.'

'Can I get him to come and find you when he's finished his meeting – I'm afraid he is tied up at the minute.'

'Look, I'm not interested in his meeting. I need him NOW. That means now. NOT in ten minutes time.'

She hovered threateningly in the hallway, a pale blue parasol twitching dangerously in one hand. I went into Louise's office, rang George's extension number and waited for the explosion.

'I said I didn't want to be disturbed,' he shouted before I had a chance to say a word, and slammed down the phone. Oh, hell, I thought. Why do these two always have to be so damn awkward?

'I'll go upstairs and get him for you, Lady

Leghorn,' I said, resigned to my fate. 'What shall I say you want him for?'

'It's FAR TOO IMPORTANT to explain to you,' she screeched. 'Get George.'

I ran up the stairs and along a maze of passages to his new office which was now housed in a distant part of the stable block.

'Yes,' he barked as I knocked warily on the door.

'I'm sorry to butt in but we've got her ladyship downstairs making a terrible fuss, insisting on seeing you. Something vitally important she says.'

He excused himself from his meeting and charged back down the passage from where I had just come.

'Ah, Lady Leghorn, good morning,' I heard him bellow from the top of the stairs.

'George, darling,' she shrieked in return. 'It's so kind of you to come down but I've got to have a quick word with you before his lordship comes over.' Suddenly she was all charm and delight. 'I need just a tiny little bit of money transferred to my house opening account and it's got to be done today or it'll get overdrawn, which I absolutely won't have, as you know.'

George, used to these gushing, flirtatious outbursts, was not easily persuaded.

'I know you don't like getting overdrawn, Lady Leghorn, but why is it about to get overdrawn? Surely the income at the moment is good – it's the height of the tourist season.'

Stating the obvious was treading on dangerous ground and I sensed that he was angling for an argument having been disturbed from his meeting.

26

'I've had some gorgeous little sofas re-upholstered,' she explained, smiling coyly and placing her hand on his arm. 'You know, those terribly valuable ones by Chippendale in the Gainsborough room. Very precious to his lordship and worth an absolute fortune.'

'Well I'm afraid the estate account isn't in a position to help at the moment, Lady Leghorn, it's a bad time for the cashflow.'

She just ignored him and continued.

'But if you just transfer some money it makes the house opening account so much more profitable, don't you see?' Her ladyship's business management did not necessarily conform to normal accounting procedure and this was often the cause of some tense situations, one of which was imminent.

'I'm afraid I don't see, Lady Leghorn. It doesn't make anything more profitable – it's taking money out of one pot and putting it in another. It's about as useful as rearranging the deckchairs on the *Titanic*. It'll make no difference whatsoever.'

'We've got to have it from somewhere. George. I don't care where. Just please DO it.'

'How much is it?'

'Twenty thousand pounds.'

'Twenty thousand pounds,' he repeated in disbelief, 'on doing up some chairs.'

'Sofas,' she said crossly, 'not chairs. And it includes a few other expenses as well. Anyway I'm in a great hurry so I'll leave it with you, George. I CANNOT discuss this any more.' She turned on her stiletto heel and walked out of the office.

'Bloody woman,' he swore under his breath. 'James, have a look at the account balances and transfer some money to sort it out for the time being.'

So I telephoned the bank and then settled back down at my desk where I had been preparing some plans for renovating a derelict cottage in Harbottle, one of the estate hamlets. The cottage, a pretty stone-and-thatch building unused for many years, required a complete modernisation scheme. Some of the measurements I'd taken on a previous visit did not quite tally so I rang through to Sophie, the pre-college office assistant, to ask her to help me measure up on site that afternoon.

'Hi, Sophie, what are you doing after lunch?' I asked her.

'I was going to check all the time sheets from the building staff.'

'Well, do you want to do something far more interesting and help me re-measure the thatched cottage at Harbottle?'

A pretty, slim, dark-haired girl called Sophie had come to the estate office to undertake a year's work experience before going off to college and had become a capable and competent member of the team.

Along with the plans it was necessary to prepare a detailed specification of the building works so that contractors could price the work accurately and I had begun dictating this when his lordship walked in.

'Good morning, James,' he said, his speech slightly slurred by the stroke he had suffered some years earlier. 'I-I'm not d-disturbing you, am I?'

I stood up. 'No, not at all my lord, come in.'

'I wanted to talk to you about s-security here,' he said. 'I'm afraid t-that I f-found Ben Rosewell asleep again the other night.'

Ben Rosewell was one of the nightwatchmen and the fact that his lordship had found him asleep for the third time in a fortnight did not bode well for his long-term employment on the estate. House security was a constant headache and unfortunately it was proving difficult to appoint a new person to the job. Mr Rosewell was a temporary solution while I interviewed others.

'Oh, dear, not again, my lord. It's terribly awkward but we've got to keep him for now or we'd be completely without. I am interviewing two people tomorrow though. Let's hope one of them may be okay.'

'Ah, good, yes,' he said, 'let's hope s-so, let's hope so,' and he wandered off, presumably to talk to Louise.

Lord Leghorn took a great interest in estate matters and was said to be familiar with everything that went on. He had a remarkable memory for names and details and often surprised me with his knowledge of the tenants' families on all the estates. His interest generally leant towards the more trivial side of things while complicated land deals or tax planning held little appeal, which was why I suppose, at that moment, a parrot was occupying most of his lordship's time. Ironically another parrot, in a separate incident, was wasting a lot of mine.

According to the reports I'd received, his lordship had been awakened one morning by a lot of screeching outside his bedroom window where, upon inspection, he had apparently seen a blue-and-red parrot perched in the rose garden. After this had gone on for three days in a row he could stand it no longer and the issue of the parrot was raised in one of our management meetings. These meetings, held fortnightly in his lordship's study, were designed to discuss matters of estate policy and to advise him on management decisions. Chatting about minor issues frustrated George so it was fortunate that he was away on this particular occasion.

'Bloody t-thing wakes me up every d-day,' he explained. 'Could you get Gribble to s-shoot it, d'you think?' Gribble was the head gamekeeper whose ability with pheasants, partridges and ducks was well known. I personally doubted that it extended to parrots.

'I'll see what we can do m'lord – you say it's in the rose garden every day at eight o'clock in the morning?' I asked.

'Yes, that's right,' he said, 'eight o'clock.'

Not having the faintest idea about catching parrots I telephoned the Russetshire Caged Bird Society and spoke to their secretary, a Mr Ogwama.

'You just leave it to me, man. I know these birds. It's in my mind how they fly,' he assured me. After a somewhat complicated discussion concerning sunflower seeds and cuttlefish he offered to come and help.

True to his word, Mr Ogwama arrived at the

estate office at seven o'clock the following morning clutching a long pole with a net on the end. 'Man, what a spread,' he enthused. 'This sure is one hell of a pad.' He wasn't quite what I had been expecting. I had imagined someone less colourful in both voice and dress. Thinking of the parrot I reflected that perhaps like attracted like. I left him concealed in a shrubbery next to the rose garden to wait for the results.

They were dramatic. Within the hour the house was surrounded by police. I rushed outside to find the tall Rastafarian being dragged out of the bushes and a policeman saying, 'Well, I've heard 'em all now, looking for a parrot, I ask you?'

'What's going on?' I asked.

'Had a call from the house, sir, about a suspicious man in the grounds and found this gentleman lurking in the bushes.'

'Ah, I see,' I retorted. 'Actually, he's supposed to be there. He's trying to catch a parrot.'

The policeman stared at me in disbelief until I had explained the situation. After apologising to Mr Ogwama and making a statement to the police, I visited the house and the drama was resolved. However, it took all my powers of persuasion to get Mr Ogwama to return the following day. The episode ended happily though when the bird was caught in his net and I, along with his lordship, was relieved as peace returned to the rose garden.

The other parrot with which I was involved at that time was very real, loud and obnoxious. It was called Joey and had a rather chequered history. He had obviously been kept by some

31

pretty rough sorts in his day but now resided with a close friend of the earl, the elderly Miss Pearson. She was a frail old lady in poor health and his lordship had asked me to take an interest in her affairs.

She lived in a large country house on the edge of the estate with the parrot, which sat in a cage in a corner of her drawing room, shouting obscenities at her visitors. It seemed that Miss Pearson had led such a sheltered life she was unaware of the vulgarity of the bird's language. Indeed it was rumoured that she thought it originated from Dutch Indonesia on the basis that much of its vocabulary sounded Flemish. All I ever heard it say was, 'Shut the f**king door then,' but I understood its repertoire was considerably larger.

When Miss Pearson fell and her broken hip required hospital attention, her housekeeper – a Mrs Cowan – kindly took in the parrot. All should have worked well but in the event Miss Pearson never returned and moved to an old people's home in Russet. Her one request was that she should be able to have Joey accompany her. The bird duly went off to the nursing home but was evicted soon after by the matron because its obscene language upset some of the other residents. Mrs Cowan kindly took it in again. Now suffering from senile dementia, Miss Pearson claimed that Mrs Cowan had stolen it. The greatly upset housekeeper then came to see me.

My suggestion that I should wring its neck did not go down as well as I'd hoped. By this time I was spending more hours than I wished on Miss Pearson's affairs, including the sale of her house and chattels, so I was not overly keen on becoming further embroiled with Joey's plight. However, after some diplomatic negotiations, Joey remained with Mrs Cowan and, spending some of Miss Pearson's inheritance, I purchased a replica Joey, which, as far as I know, still resides in the nursing home in Russet. The new Joey never uttered a word, which pleased matron and perplexed Miss Pearson, while the old Joey had expanded his vocabulary. When I last saw him, he screeched, inaccurately I hope, 'Smells of pee,' which I imagine he picked up during his short sojourn in the nursing home.

## Chapter 4

The inter-office telephone rang and I picked it up.

'James, will you come up to my office straightaway please?' barked George in annoyance.

I wound my way along the passages to his vast office which was as usual in total disarray, papers, files and plans scattered haphazardly all over the place. Despite the chaos there was no doubt that he was a good land agent who had both an excellent eye for detail and a ruthlessness that achieved results.

'Right, morning, James,' he started brusquely. 'I want you to let me have a list of the farm rent reviews that you've prepared, you don't seem to be making much progress with them. And I also want the agenda prepared for our management meeting with his lordship next Monday.'

I started to explain why the reviews were taking so long but he cut me off.

'I'm not interested. Just get on with them and if you've got to stay here all night then do it.'

I shrugged my shoulders and resisted the urge to bite back.

'Have you got anything you want included on the agenda?' I asked instead, knowing that he considered these meetings with his lordship a waste of valuable time.

'Oh, God,' he said, 'I suppose I'd better think of something to include. What have we got so far?'

'It's a bit short at the moment. The fire practice and Rose Cottage, Upper Maplethorpe.'

'World shattering events as usual. Well, it'll have to do so bring me a copy when Lou's typed it will you?'

These meetings would be held in Lord Leghorn's study every other Monday at 11.30 am, the aim being to keep his lordship in touch with events on the estate. However, there was a flaw in this thinking because the more important items were usually so complicated and boring that his lordship tended to skim over them, preferring to concentrate on issues that appealed to him. George would get desperately frustrated trying to explain a million-pound development deal when all his lordship wanted to know was whether we had stopped the deer getting on to the cricket pitch.

Not much later George went out for the remainder of the day and with the Leghorns firmly entrenched in their London flat I managed to make good progress on my work.

At about one o'clock I decided to pop home for some lunch and so told Lou not to expect me back until half-past two as I would be calling in at Mrs Elliot's to discuss her lavatory before my return. Many of the estate cottages were sorely in need of modernisation but some of the elderly tenants, Mrs Elliot included, held some rather unorthodox views which hindered progress. For some reason she maintained that to have a lavatory inside the house was unhygienic and it was far healthier to have a 'bucket and chuck it' arrangement in the garden. The Environmental Health officer from the district council held a different view and had been trying to persuade her to reconsider. Her cottage, along with several others on the estate, still had a small brick-built shed at the bottom of the garden. This contained a wooden box with a hole cut in the top, an earth floor and a distinctly unsavoury smell. Of course, as Mrs Elliot pointed out, one of the great advantages of that kind of system was that there was nothing that could break down. Once a week you simply went to the little door at the back of the shed and emptied the box with a shovel. I never asked her where she put the contents but I had noticed that she maintained a particularly productive vegetable garden. Indeed she had won the 'biggest marrow' competition at the Bassett Horticultural show for many years.

My house was a couple of miles from the office

on a small sheep farm that I rented from the estate. I had held a practical interest in farming since I was a boy and when the opportunity had arisen for me to rent the farm I had jumped at it. At first, George and his lordship considered that it would involve me in too much extra work and dilute my efforts elsewhere on the estate, but when I assured them that this wouldn't happen and pointed out that it would give me a greater reason to be nearby at weekends and holidays they changed their opinion.

'Much better he's here with his hand up a sheep's backside than down in London chasing girls along the Kings Road,' George explained to his lordship. 'At least he's here if there's a problem.'

And the situation had turned out very well. I loved having a different reason for settling down in the area apart from my work, especially as I lived on my own. It gave me something else to do when I wasn't in the office and, with the help of a part-time shepherd, I coped easily.

I had just finished my lunch when the phone rang.

'James, it's Lou. I hoped I'd catch you before you left for Mrs Elliot's.'

'Oh, dear, what's happened?' I asked, knowing that she would only ring me at home if it was something very important.

'I've had Lord Leghorn on the phone from London and he wants you to ring him straight-away.'

'Do you know what he wants?'

'No, he wouldn't say. Only that it's urgent and

he'll wait for you to ring back.'

'Presumably he's at the flat – have you got the number?'

I dialled the London number and the maid put me straight through to his lordship. I imagined something must be seriously wrong.

'My lord, it's James here,' I said.

'T-thank you for r-ringing, James. I w-wondered if you would tell Hawthorne to trim back that honeysuckle by the Bailiff's Room,' he said, 'I keep catching my hat on it.'

'Certainly, sir,' I replied, waiting with anxiety for the urgent problem that had prompted his call.

'T-thank you. Goodbye.'

I stared at the telephone in disbelief for a second, wondered why on earth that couldn't have waited for a day or two and then set off for Mrs Elliot's.

Mrs Elliot was a charming old lady in her mid-eighties, still active and with a quick mind. She had lived in the same cottage since the day she had got married sixty-five years earlier. Her late husband Fred had been the head carpenter in the days when the household staff alone numbered fifty and she would often tell me stories about the past when the previous earl was seated at Rumshott. But on this occasion her thoughts were of a more fundamental nature and I could sense that the local council man's protestations had finally been having an effect.

'Well it's not really him,' she said, aware that for years she had resisted the offer of an indoor lavatory, 'it's that I'm beginning to find the

37

digging out a bit tiresome and I don't like to ask my neighbours to do it.'

I had to agree. I did not think her neighbours would welcome the task at all.

'Well, Mrs Elliot, the plans have been ready for some time now so all we need to do is tell the builders to get on with it. How about a week on Monday?'

Having at last got her agreement I judged it prudent to get on with it before she had second thoughts.

'Yes, Mr Aden, that's ever so kind of you; in fact I'm beginning to get quite excited about it what with not having to go outside on winter nights with a torch.'

I drove back to the office with a feeling of achievement. Mrs Elliot was about to have her first indoor lavatory, which as estate villages go, was a revolutionary event.

As I returned to Rumshott I marvelled at how fortunate I was to live and work in such beautiful surroundings. The estate villages were built of attractive stone quarried locally when horses and carts had been the only form of transport. Many of the older cottages had thatched roofs and flower-filled gardens reminiscent of pictures in country calendars that one sends to aged aunts at Christmas. Out of the village the wide green fields rolled down towards the park walls, and pockets of woodland covered the steeper slopes. It was easy to understand why hundreds of years ago a Leghorn ancestor had decided to build his mansion at Rumshott.

I decided I'd better see Hawthorne about this

honeysuckle before going back into the office where some other drama was sure to make me forget it, so I parked my car at the back door of Rumshott House and went to find him. It was always useful to drop in on the staff unannounced as most of them worked without supervision and part of my job was to oversee and organise their work. Hawthorne was particularly isolated as he was the only gardener, and I had had to pay special attention to him ever since the episode when his lordship found him asleep in the potting shed, an occasion that had made a difficult relationship even more strained. The two had never got on very well in any case, a situation not helped by his lordship's unfounded but unshakeable conviction that Hawthorne's wife, who cleaned the estate office, was a spy for the Inland Revenue. Quite how that ever got into his mind I never discovered.

I found Hawthorne down by the swimming pool, for once not welded to the seat of the lawnmower, and showed him the offending honeysuckle. Despite Hawthorne's shortcomings I could always guarantee that if I asked him to do something it would be done straight away.

Having dealt with that I left the car where it was and walked through the gardens back to the office. After dictating a letter to the builder who was going to install Mrs Elliot's lavatory I was at last able to continue working on the farm rent reviews which were fast becoming a thorn in my side.

Sophie came in to help me by looking up costings for various farming activities. Her year at

Rumshott was part of her training as a land agent and she had to spend the time seeing practice. While she did get landed with a never-ending list of menial jobs I tried to get her involved with some of the professional work when it was possible. With George and the Leghorns away we were able to work through undisturbed until seven o'clock by which time we'd had enough for the day.

'Would you like to come and have some supper?' I asked her, grateful for the help she had given me and aware that her existence in the estate cottage where she lived was pretty dull. Great Bassett was hardly the most riveting place for a lively teenager.

As she looked at me her long dark eyelashes momentarily flickered and as usual I felt a ripple of desire flow through me. I let it linger for a moment before burying such thoughts. There was an unspoken acceptance between us that nothing could ever happen but I sometimes wondered if that would last. After all she was an attractive, slim, dark-haired girl of nineteen and I was a single man of twenty-six and both of us lived on our own on the estate. It was hard to put duty before pleasure, especially when she was wearing a short skirt showing off her shapely and endless legs. I felt a sudden lapse in my guard. I wanted to hold her, kiss her and feel her body against mine. For the thousandth time I wondered what I could do but as always came to the same conclusion that it wouldn't work – it would destroy the rapport we had in the office and create a difficult situation for everyone.

'Come down at about eight o'clock if you like,' I said neutrally, 'there's enough food for us both.'

Evenings with Sophie were rather like window shopping, looking but not touching the goods. The isolation of our jobs meant that we often ate supper together, which was immeasurably enjoyable but equally frustrating. I relished her company but there was an undercurrent of unease not helped by the fact that we avoided talking about the issue that kept us apart. Each evening would end early when we reached that awkward part where either you're going to spend the night together or it's time to fill up the hot-water bottle.

I rushed home and put a casserole in the oven before taking my horse, Grehan, out for a ride around the woods near Harbottle. Bramble, a black Labrador puppy, followed at heel and I relaxed for the first time that day. I marvelled at the joy of being outside on a warm June evening with my animals for company and noticed that the corn was starting to turn colour, the green now tinged with brown. The paths were thick with tall grass and a mass of wild flowers and I tried to imagine what it would be like to work in a city with the people, the noise and the pollution. As I reached the top of the hill above the woods I could see my house below me, but there were no people about, there was no noise apart from Grehan champing at her bit and the warm sweet air was filled with the scent of the hedgerow flowers.

It must be nice to be an earl, I thought, but it wasn't bad being a land agent.

# Chapter 5

The following Monday a management meeting with his lordship had been arranged. His lordship had developed a set routine for these meetings held in his study and was strangely particular over who sat in which chair. The room was richly decorated with an ornate marble fireplace at one end and a superb Georgian mahogany breakfront bookcase at the other. His desk fitted into the window bay overlooking the rose garden at the front of the house and underneath a priceless painting by Stubbs were two armchairs and a sofa. He and George would sit in these chairs while I was given a hard upright dining chair positioned between the two of them. I felt like the umpire at a tennis match sitting somewhat higher than them, and I wondered whether it reminded his lordship of the days when he used to play.

Unfortunately it was an easy room in which to relax. Apart from the lavish decor and much sought-after works of art, it was always too hot and on occasions I would drift comfortably into oblivion until abruptly startled by a question from one side or the other.

George and I walked over to the house together as always before these meetings mindful of our positions within the Leghorn entourage. We were still servants even if our professional jobs carried the responsibilities of managing the family's considerable estates. Land agents have an unusual place in the hierarchy of a landed estate, being entrusted with enormous power and relied upon for crucial advice and yet often given instructions to do things wholly inappropriate to good estate management.

Lord Leghorn held firm views on many matters but he was undoubtedly influenced by Lady Leghorn a great deal of the time. This was particularly the case when it came to discussing money because his great wealth was predominantly tied up in the estate while Lady Leghorn's interest lay in ready cash. Good estate management meant trying to keep the estate intact and inevitably when there was a cash shortage the blame fell at the agent's door. It was sometimes difficult to predict the outcome of these meetings as it depended on her ladyship's current fund requirements and these fluctuated wildly and without warning.

The whole issue of managing the Leghorn estates was further complicated by two major factors. As Lady Leghorn was his lordship's second wife and they had no children from their marriage the long-term future of the estate was of no particular concern to her. This led to the second factor, Lord Leghorn's children. Aristocratic families have an ancestry that they usually wish to preserve – the titles, stately homes, landed estates and art collections. As with most families in this situation the Leghorns established trusts to benefit future generations, in particular the heir, Viscount Rumshott. The trusts were wealthy and owned valuable land

43

holdings but vitally they did not own Rumshott House which belonged to his lordship. This exacerbated the cash problem, as the cost of running the house was phenomenal, and the Leghorns' lavish lifestyle meant that it was necessary to sell a few of his lordship's assets from time to time in order to smooth things over.

The family difficulties were an ever-present problem but on this occasion the meeting did not contain any contentious items. The first one merely reported the forthcoming sale of a cottage in Upper Maplethorpe which had already been earmarked for disposal and would provide some income for the estate. Sales were always a good item to start the meetings off as his lordship saw them as an easy way to get some ready cash. He owned so many houses that I suppose he felt that selling the odd one off here and there wouldn't make much difference. However, his views when it came to other people owning property were strange.

'D-did you know that Simmonds,' who was one of the estate's solicitors, 'owns a v-villa in Spain?' he asked with incredulity. 'It s-seems extra-ordinary t-that people can afford to have more than one house. He must be terribly rich.'

He was genuinely surprised and thought that it was excessively extravagant. George started to explain that Simmonds probably bought it as an investment as much as for holidays but I felt that he was wasting his time. His lordship obviously did not have much concept of relative values. Here was a man who lived with his wife in a house the size of a small town, and they did not

44

even have a cat! He owned over a hundred cottages in the area and a luxury flat in the heart of London.

The last item to be discussed was the fire practice, seemingly a straightforward little task that I arranged with the Russetshire fire service on a regular but infrequent basis. However, since a disastrous fire at Hampton Court Palace the earl had taken a more active role in these arrangements, which I am afraid caused major complications. His lordship had apparently sat next to Her Majesty The Queen at a dinner and evidently she had explained in graphic detail the terrible damage suffered to the palace and as a result he now felt it was his duty to be fully involved in the fire practices at Rumshott.

'I t-think it is t-time that we tried out the fire engine with the extending ladder,' he suggested, 'and s-see if it's capable of reaching the attic windows.'

He had seen this vehicle driving around Russet a while ago and mentioned it to me at the time. He must have had it in the back of his mind ever since.

'And to make the w-whole thing more realistic,' he continued, 'the fire b-brigade can bring s-some of those smoke bombs which we can let off up there on the top staircase.'

George glanced at me and I could sense that unless we were careful it would get out of hand.

'If we get a d-dummy the object of the p-practice can be to rescue it using the extending ladder.'

'Well we'll sort it out, m'lord,' interrupted

45

George who was clearly getting concerned. 'Of course a lot will depend on what the fire officer will agree to do,' he added.

It was going to develop into a real-life drama just trying to organise the event and as if to reinforce my thoughts his lordship stated:

'And we'll do it during house opening hours to see how the guides cope with the tourists.'

Bearing in mind that most of the guides who showed visitors around the house were elderly gentlefolk that Lady Leghorn had gathered from the surrounding villages it was obvious right from the start that it would end in chaos.

Nonetheless we selected a date and I was left to organise the practice. It was a serious matter and the fire drill at Rumshott had been worked out many years before with the full cooperation of the fire brigade. In the event of a fire the newly installed comprehensive alarm system automatically alerted the fire station. Due to the large size of the house the system was split into zones, which were indicated on the control panel by the back door and which directed the firemen to the relevant areas.

The first priority was to evacuate people from the building and then to concentrate on rescuing pictures from the Long Gallery which contained the most valuable of the Rumshott art collection. This room was 140 feet long and ran along the west side of the house at first floor level. It was a difficult room to access and to make matters worse there was a particularly large Van Dyck painting, which must have been twelve feet by twenty, covering the end wall. This piece of art was destined to be the first saved in the case of a fire and one of the windows had been especially altered so that the picture could be removed through it on a special winch and lowered to the ground outside. The picture was a great issue, particularly as his lordship always insisted that it should be rescued before worrying about the people because it was irreplaceable.

I knew he looked forward to fire practices with excitement and on the day he would rush about indulging in his passion for photography taking pictures, a hobby at which he was exceptionally talented. So I was rather surprised on the day before it was all due to take place to receive one of his memos, which appeared when his lordship had something of importance to record. They were typed on most distinctive pieces of paper that he ordered from Smythson's of Bond Street in London, beautifully edged in colour and watermarked. He typed them himself with im-precision on an ancient typewriter.

The memo read:

*To: James Aden*
*From: Lord Leghorn*
*Many thanks for arranging a Fire Practice here in daylight on Oct. 31st. I am sorry to say we shall not be at home on that day. Will you please give me a written report after the practice?*

*I enclose a relevant piece from the agenda of a charity with which I am conected. There may be lessons to be learnt from this fire drill in an old people's home: anyway I thought it would amuse you.*

And attached to it was the following:
*Fire drills*

47

*To note that Miss Bennett had a fire drill at the house at 8pm. in the evening of Wednesday 13th September, i.e. not during daylight. She was pleased that with the exception of two ladies the house was vacated within five minutes. However, Miss Ridley fell in the darkness outside and had to be taken to Casualty, not returning until 1am.*

*Miss Bennett feels that:*

*1. Such a fire drill should not be repeated in the dark.*

*2. The alarm bells need to be much louder.*

*3. The corridor doors should be left open as the ladies are finding it more and more difficult to push them open.*

*Note: One lady from the top floor said plaintively, 'What am I doing out here? I only wanted the commode.'*

I suspected that we may well have similar problems of our own.

At the appointed time I crept up the back stairs carrying the dummy and a smoke canister provided by the fire brigade, set the thing off and scuttled downstairs to activate the fire alarm.

With deafening blasts the sirens wailed and I watched to see how smoothly or not the evacuation plan would be followed. It was not. The house staff ran about like headless chickens clearly unaware of what they were supposed to do and when I went through into the state rooms where the public were present it was pure farce.

Most of the visitors stood rooted to the spot with their hands over their ears while one ancient lady whom I recognised as a guide had collapsed on to a Louis XV elbow chair in a state of shock. Other guides were trying to help an elderly gentleman whose wheelchair had become stuck in the fire exit.

Needless to say the firemen were not impressed with the situation that greeted their arrival and I was given strict instructions to prepare a revised fire evacuation drill.

His lordship was not at all happy either when he received my written report and the new plan became a matter of great urgency. It had to cover the evacuation of any people in the house and a system of rescuing some of the paintings. It involved preparing a plan of the whole building showing evacuation routes and access points for the firemen. It turned out to be a long and complicated project.

## Chapter 6

Sorting out the fire procedures may have been tedious but it wasn't anywhere near as irritating as the issue of the blue gate. The blue gate had been causing me a lot of trouble over the last couple of months, all of it Lady Leghorn's doing. The problem, centred around the paying visitors coming to the house and Lady Leghorn's insistence that they be diverted through her gift shop. The public car park was behind the stable block, where we and estate office visitors also parked, and normally one could then walk underneath the stable block archway to the office or on to the house. The tea room and gift shop were situated along one length of the block, converted from a range of stables, and Lady Leghorn's theory was that if the blue gate under the arch was kept locked then the tourists would be compelled to enter via the shop. This was a fine marketing ploy but it was a damned nuisance for us as we were always popping in and out, and also for people calling at the estate office on business. So we tended to leave the gate open until her ladyship noticed, at which point she would come storming into the office and make us lock it up. The result was that our visitors were often found wandering around the gift shop with Lady Leghorn's helpers trying to sell them Rumshott fudge.

When Lady Leghorn issued instructions they tended to be obeyed. The blue gate was a minor irritation but when these irritations built up into a major problem then that meant trouble. Somehow she managed to cause huge disruptions to the smooth running of the estate and create havoc for nearly all the estate staff. There was also the difficulty of how her projects were to be paid for since projects would be under way before anyone knew where the money was coming from. As her ideas tended to cost tens, if not hundreds, of thousands of pounds there was always a drama over the money.

The Red House was a classic example and, as with all these projects came about because Lady Leghorn was bored. The object of many of her schemes seemed to be to pass the time while she was in residence at Rumshott in the same way that other people might carry out some 'do it yourself' in their homes. It would have been fine if she'd pottered off to B&Q and bought a sheet of plywood and a tin of paint but she operated on a rather different scale. The Red House was situated in the park and although it had been built in quite a grand style it was in fact the head gardener's cottage in the days when the gardens employed dozens of staff. Hawthorne lived in the village by preference and the cottage had been used until recently by Lord Leghorn's daughters as a holiday retreat.

When they gave it up it should, from a financial point of view, simply have been re-let in the same way as any of the other hundred or so cottages on the estate. But her ladyship chose to employ probably the most famous, and certainly the most expensive interior designers in the country to redesign the interior. Then the builders moved in, bringing with them electricians, plumbers, kitchen specialists, bathroom specialists and decorators. Money poured out of the estate account as the work progressed and despite various attempts by George to thwart it, Lady Leghorn ploughed on relentlessly. Lavish fabrics from Colefax and Fowler arrived, the highest quality Wilton carpets were laid, and antique furniture and expensive paintings were collected until finally the house was completed.

There were two factors that she had failed to take into account. First, no one wanted to rent it at the rate now appropriate and second, over £100,000 had disappeared from the estate account, which had not been budgeted for at the

51

beginning of the year. Then the rows erupted over where the money was going to come from and the relationship between her and the estate office became strained. The house was eventually let to a wealthy businessman, but as George pointed out to her at the time, we could have got nearly the same rent from someone else without having spent any money on it at all.

Lord Leghorn tended to steer clear of these rows, preferring to let her ladyship get on with it despite the damage to the bank balance. Instead he would make small savings elsewhere, although it wasn't always easy to consider his efforts significantly helpful.

During the Red House fiasco he arrived in the office carrying an umbrella, to report some excellent news.

'D-do you know,' he said, 'I was given this umbrella absolutely free in Harrods yesterday!'

'Well, that's amazing, my lord. I expect it'll come in useful when it rains!' I didn't know what else to say except perhaps that considering the amount of money he must spend in the shop they ought to give him a free umbrella every time he went in. It turned out that it was not actually free, because the following week a bill arrived from the store for a £900 television set, which he had bought in order to get the free umbrella. It might have been more understandable had he actually needed a new television.

However, it wasn't only his lordship who came up with unusual money-saving ideas. I suggested that it would be extremely valuable to ride Grehan around the estate as it would give me a different perspective on Rumshott. I admit it was a purely selfish interest but the sense of it was well received, to my surprise, by both George and Lord Leghorn. One missed such a lot of detail driving around in the car and yet walking took far too much time, so by horse it became. The only hiccup in my plan occurred when Lady Leghorn discovered Hawthorne cleaning out the stable next to my office where I intended to park the horse during the day. Unfortunately the stable was also near to her shop. Very protective of her retail enterprise, she declared that the presence of a horse nearby would frighten her customers away. Hawthorne, pleased not to have to clean out the stable, for once wholeheartedly agreed with her.

However, his lordship was so keen on the idea of having a horse about the place that the stable was duly made available.

Often during the day I would ride out to wherever the estate workers were to be found to see how they were progressing. Riding proved to be an excellent form of transport and I began to cover many acres of the estate on Grehan's back.

It was paradise. I had 8,500 acres over which to roam and the rolling countryside was beautiful and varied. I had my favourite places to go, the park itself, Harbottle woods and the wide meadow valleys stretching between the Bassetts and the Addiscombe hills.

The park alone covered five hundred acres and was full of interesting features such as the high grassy banks surrounding Rumshott House and its gardens. At the highest point in the park were the old kitchen gardens next to the Red House which Lady Leghorn had had renovated. The gardens were enclosed by ancient redbrick walls ten or twelve feet high and although disused it was easy to imagine the large team of gardeners which had tended those sheltered acres in order to provide enough food for the mansion. Leading from there was a series of spring-fed lakes which followed the valley floor towards the house and the oval lake in the arboretum. In the summer, Grehan would wade in to the shallows and cool her legs while I would watch the colourful dragonflies darting about on the surface of the water. Sometimes a fish might make a splash as it leapt for a fly. Then there were many small clumps of woodland dotted around the park, one of which contained the Icehouse, another relic of the past. This was the underground cave in which blocks of ice cut from the lakes during the winter would be stored until they were needed by the house. It was sealed off with a menacing-looking iron grill as it had become dangerous and all that was visible now was a brick entrance tunnel which was almost completely shrouded by ferns and thorn trees.

At each entrance to the park were the gate lodges, built in the local sand-coloured stone and forming part of the park walls. They straddled the massive decorative wrought-iron gates that could be closed to seal Rumshott off from the outside world.

At the far end of the park, well away from the prying eyes of the public and press was the Folly, Viscount Rumshott's home. Originally constructed as a folly the building was basically a single room built above a grandiose vaulted hall containing a wide stone staircase leading to a viewing platform. In the Victorian era the building had been converted into a house while a rear wing which contained the kitchens and extra bedrooms had since been added. Edward Rumshott used it as his country retreat and often came down at weekends to entertain groups of friends.

At the very northern corner of the park there was a huge heronry where a great flock of these tall graceful birds nested in the tops of the trees in a secluded area of woodland protected by the park walls. But the most serene and tranquil place to spend some time was in the arboretum beside Rumshott House. There was a fascinating collection of rare and interesting trees while a wide gravel path led through them to the oval lake, a hidden corner of the estate where one could rest for a while and spend some quiet moments in thought. The only likely disturbance would be from the wild ducks and other birds that nested on the island in the middle of the lake.

Although most of the features of the park were man made, they had existed for so many hundreds of years that it seemed their existence graced the surroundings with a natural permanence. To ride around the park on Grehan was to be reminded of the historical association between the aristocracy and the land and was a powerful enough experience to warrant many explorations.

If I wanted a different type of scenery then I would sometimes take Grehan up into Harbottle woods and canter along the wide grassy rides, perhaps stopping in an open glade to let her munch some grass. These woods were a mixture of broad-leaved woodlands containing mainly oak, ash and hazel and had probably been in existence since before the first Leghorn had built his mansion at Rumshott. A perpetual carpet of wild flowers, at its most glorious in late May when the floor became a dense purple haze of bluebells, lay underneath the trees. Their scent filled the spring air on a warm evening and it was usually up that you could hear the first cuckoo of summer.

For a fast gallop where I could let Grehan have her head and experience the thrill of riding a horse at its utmost speed I would go into the grass valleys heading towards the Addiscombe hills. I could ride through pastures uninterrupted by the plough for these were ancient sheep-grazed fields with safe, solid turf – perfect for a galloping horse.

At the top of Addiscombe Hill itself was a tenant farmer of my own age who had become one of my few friends on the estate. It was difficult to make proper friends as deputy agent because one was always aware of the potential for landlord-tenant conflict. It could be a lonely job knowing that there was this invisible barrier and so I particularly valued Tom Dagg's friendship.

If I had the time I would call in at his yard, leave Grehan in a loose box and have a cup of tea or a beer in the farmhouse kitchen with him. He was a bachelor like myself and we shared a similar outlook on life although I was perhaps more houseproud than my friend. I liked to be comfortable and had someone from the village come in and keep the place clean for me but when you visited Tom's house it was difficult to tell whether or not you were still in the yard. The floor was permanently littered with straw and unidentifiable objects, some of which used occasionally to move. During one visit I found a rubber castration ring, used to remove lambs' testicles, at the bottom of my cup of tea.

## Chapter 7

I suppose that if I had been working in London or some other large city, social invitations from people hoping to do business with the estate would have been commonplace. However, stuck out in the middle of the countryside such occasions were almost non-existent so it was very exciting to be asked to attend a local point-to-point as a guest of a firm called Be-warm. Be-warm supplied the estate with heating oil so going along to an amateur race meeting with them didn't have quite the same cachet as being invited by Courts and Co. to luncheon at Claridge's but nonetheless it was a start. There was a cold buffet lunch and plenty of alcohol promised presumably to encourage us to sign some agreement binding the estate to buying their kerosene for the next ten years.

To my surprise and delight I found that Sophie, who ordered the weekly oil deliveries, had also been asked. Be-warm kindly sent a car to collect us. It was a beautiful spring day early in April, the sort of day when the smell of the warm earth and early blossoms promise that love is in the air and a young man's attentions may turn to mating.

By the time Sophie and I arrived at their marquee beside the racecourse I doubt that any of the Be-warm staff could have told the difference between a can of kerosene and a glass of Chardonnay. The party was in full swing and the reps who looked after the Leghorn account rushed over to attend to our every need. There were a few local farmers there that I knew – Be-warm customers like ourselves – but as the afternoon progressed it became obvious that Sophie and I were the guests of honour. I suspect that this had more to do with the amount of oil we ordered, for which we had to thank Lady Leghorn, rather than our personalities but nonetheless the attention was flattering.

"'Ere, 'ave you put a bet on the second race yet, James?' asked Michael Pigton, the managing director of Be-warm.

'No, I haven't, Michael,' I replied, quickly glancing down at my race card. 'Have you got any hot tips?'

'Ha ha,' he laughed, 'that's our business, being hot, innit!' He shook my arm in a show of enthusiastic humour but being about six pints behind him I wasn't quite able to break into the same great convulsions of raucous laughter.

'Yes, I suppose it is,' I said 'Ha ha.' I tried laughing politely but when I realised that I was making a sound like an egg-bound chicken, I

58

gave up.

'What about number fourteen,' I suggested. 'Everywhichway – seems to have won a bit before.'

'That'll do. I ain't got a bloody clue to be honest wiv you mate. One 'orse looks the same as another to me,' he informed me, helpfully.

I looked at Sophie who was staring at Mr Pigton with bemusement.

'Sophie!' I said.

She jumped. 'What?' she asked.

'Any ideas on a good bet for the second?'

She was a competent rider and her father rode in point-to-points so I thought that she might have some useful hints. 'How about Rancid Roger?'

'Name doesn't inspire much does it?'

'No but it's being ridden by Tom Sheldrick who's a pretty successful jockey. I don't think he'd take a ride on a no-hoper.'

'Okay, you go for him and I'll try Every-whichway.'

We pushed our way through the crowds along the bookies' line trying to find the one offering the best odds.

'Put a fiver on each and I'll double it for you to a tenner,' chirped Mr Pigton from behind. 'Can't say Be-warm don't look after you, can we?'

'That's very kind of you Mr Pigton,' said Sophie. 'Who gets the winnings though?' She laughed.

'You do, my love,' he replied, leering at her through a drunken haze.

Everywhichway was running at 5-1 and Rancid Roger at 20-1.

'Yours is a bit of a long shot,' I remarked as the £10 note was handed over. 'Still, two hundred quid if it wins!'

We wandered back to the hospitality marquee from which there was an excellent view of the course.

''Ere you are, loves,' said a brassy looking blonde as she handed us each another glass of Pimm's. I couldn't help glancing at her generous helping of cleavage as she leant towards me and wondered how PR girls at promotional events always seemed to have such ample assets in that department.

'So that's what you look for in a woman, is it?' whispered Sophie in my ear. 'I saw you!'

'Well I could hardly miss it, could I? And no, that's not my cup of tea.'

'So what is?' she teased, the Pimm's beginning to take an effect on her normally reticent character.

'Um, someone who's slim, tall, probably long dark hair. Blue eyes, um, straight nose, high cheekbones...' She punched me as I tried to finish describing her.

'You bastard,' she joked.

'No. I'm serious,' I said.

She muttered something under her breath.

'What was that?'

'Doesn't matter. Come on, let's watch this race.'

The racecourse sprawled in front of us laid out in a valley between the Russetshire hills and from where we stood the whole circuit was visible. At the far end of the valley a brightly coloured group of jockeys milled about on their horses waiting for the starter's orders. Rancid Roger, a grey, was easily discernible from the bays and chestnuts but from that distance I couldn't make out Everywhichway.

Suddenly the loud speakers crackled into action.

'They're under starter's orders ... and they're off.'

The crowds moved towards the rails as the horses sped along the track followed by the echoing commentary of a retired colonel over the public address system.

After they had galloped past us on the first lap, my attention was drawn to the surroundings in which I found myself. The crowd was clearly enjoying the warmth of the sunshine and the excitement of the race, some avidly clutching binoculars focused on the distant horses, others sat on tartan rugs amongst an array of hampers and bottles of wine. In the far distance the outline of the Oxfordshire hills seemed to shimmer in a slight haze as the warmth from the earth drifted upwards. The shires in all their glory stretched in front of me and I was struck by the way in which the setting seemed to be so quintessentially English.

I glanced over at Sophie whose attention was focused entirely on the horses now approaching us for the second and final lap. The fine features of her face were clearly lit by the afternoon sun and the concentration emphasised her arresting beauty. Tall, slim and graceful she seemed oblivious to the admiring glances of passers-by and I thought for the thousandth time how unfair it was that we couldn't be together. I wondered again whether it really would cause a problem in the office if we went out together or whether I was just inventing excuses in order to protect my freedom. Whatever, I couldn't have it both ways.

The roar of the crowd interrupted my useless thoughts and I watched the field approaching the fence nearest to us. Sophie's Rancid Roger was lying a close second to the leader and the cries of the spectators rose to a crescendo as they screamed for their preferred winner. I watched Everywhichway doing it his way as the back-marker and turned my attention to cheering Rancid Roger home to a half-length's win.

Sophie, her blue eyes alight with excitement, flung her arms around me. 'He's won, he's won. What a brilliant finish!' she cried.

I laughed and hugged her. 'Congratulations! You've obviously got a good eye for a horse. And two hundred pounds better off so the drinks are on you!'

'It's amazing,' she said, letting go of me. 'I've never won so much before. Come on, let's go and collect my winnings.'

We ran back through the crowd, Sophie clutching her orange betting slip while others dejectedly tore theirs in half, dropping them on the ground. 'Well done, love,' said the man standing on the bookie's box who handed her the money. 'Good odds on that one – have an eye for a winner then?' He doffed his trilby at Sophie and chuckling he added to me,

'And I see you've an eye for a pretty filly, sir!'

We left him to his banter and returned to the

buxom blonde for a celebratory drink.

'We 'ave done you proud today,' greeted Mr Pigton. 'Looked after you and made you a couple of hundred quid.'

'I know. It's so exciting. We're having a wonderful day, thank you so much,' replied Sophie happily as he moved away to greet another guest.

'Shall we go and watch the next race from the top of the hill,' she suggested.

'Yeah, good idea,' I agreed. 'We'll take our drinks and sit on that bank up there.'

Finding a place on a grassy bank above the enclosure and away from the melee of racegoers we sipped our drinks in companionable silence. The effect of the warm sun and the Pimm's did nothing to help sustain my reservations about Sophie. She stretched her long slender legs in front of her and as her dark hair kept blowing in tendrils across her face in the slight breeze, she would flick it away with a toss of her head.

'Isn't this the most gorgeous day,' she said sleepily. 'I could just lie here for ever.' She sank back on the grass, the outline of her slim body discernible through the thin cotton dress.

I put my glass down and leant back on one elbow.

'Yup, I could too,' I agreed and without thinking reached forward to brush away another wayward strand of hair off her face. As I did so our eyes met and it seemed the most natural thing in the world to kiss her. It was a tentative, questioning gesture but within seconds we were embracing hungrily, clutching each other tightly, pressed together until there was no breath in us.

'Wow,' we both said in unison and laughed nervously. There was an awkward silence. 'Um – sorry. I, er, couldn't help it,' I said.

She just looked at me for a moment and then pulled me back towards her, our lips touching again, desperate for more.

For the rest of the afternoon I felt as though I was in a dream. The situation on the drive home seemed so different to how it had been when we set out in the morning and our driver had a difficult task trying to engage us in conversation, lost as we were in our own thoughts.

I had already invited Sophie to a dinner party that evening and the car dropped her off at her cottage so that she could get changed. I continued on to Harbottle wondering what the hell I had done. A huge part of me felt racked with guilt and yet at the same time my stomach was churning with excited anticipation.

The party was a great success and six friends were staying for the remainder of the weekend so there was a relaxed atmosphere in the house. The warm weather had brought on a sudden urge to devour copious quantities of chilled Chablis so once the others had disappeared off to bed, leaving Sophie and me alone downstairs, my thoughts of caution had disappeared. We curled up on the big squashy sofa in front of the dying embers of the fire and embraced with a passion built on months of pent-up frustration.

Not knowing what answer I wanted I held her head in my hands, tracing the profile of her face with my fingers.

'Do you want to stay here tonight?' I asked her.

I could feel my heart pounding as I waited for the reply. She didn't answer but stood up and holding my hand led me upstairs.

The dappled moonlight filtered through the bedroom window gently illuminating our bodies as we undressed each other. I could feel her smooth perfect skin on mine as we kissed and running my hands over her firm buttocks she pushed hard against me.

Something was happening, something totally unexpected and unplanned but I couldn't help noticing that the soft yellow moonlight was being intermittently broken by flashes of blue light.

Surely, Sophie couldn't be as electrifying as this, I thought as a great commotion erupted downstairs with dogs barking madly.

'What the hell's going on?' I cried, letting go of Sophie.

Grabbing some clothes I peered out of the window to see a police car in the yard, and PC Stan Cripps pacing up and down.

'What the hell's Stan Cripps doing here?' I said.

'Cripps!' she exclaimed. 'What a time to come.'

'Telling me!'

'What're you going to do?'

'I'll have to go and see what he wants, I suppose. Why don't you get into bed – I'll be back in a minute.'

I tore downstairs and opened the door.

'Stan, what the hell are you doing here in the middle of the night?' I demanded angrily.

'Oh, hello, James,' he replied cheerily, 'sorry to bother you. Not interrupting anything am I?'

'Course you bloody are! What's the problem?

65

Something at the house?'

'No, no. I've come to tell you that there's a load of sheep out on the main road. I'm afraid I've already woken Mr Sparkes who says the bloody things are yours, as he put it.'

'Damn, damn, damn.'

'Well, bring Jess, that sheepdog of yours and I'll help you get 'em back,' he offered. It was all part of a rural policeman's duty I supposed but to me it was an unmitigated disaster.

'Okay, Stan, that's very kind of you. I'll nip in and put some more clothes on. Hold on a minute.'

I ran back upstairs to tell Sophie the bad news. She was lying in my bed and a pang of irrepressible longing flooded through me.

'What is it?' she asked

'The bloody sheep are out,' I said.

She sat up, inadvertently exposing her small firm breasts which was something I could have done without just at that moment.

'I'll come and help,' she said, swinging her long, desirable legs out of the bed and standing naked beside me. I grabbed her and held her against me for a second.

'Thanks but don't worry. Stan'll help and I'll take Jess. You try and get some sleep.'

'Yeah. That's just what I feel like now,' she moaned. 'I think for some reason I might be a tiny bit restless!'

I looked at her aghast. 'I know. This is a real bugger, isn't it? Talk about bad timing. I'll be as quick as I can.' I kissed her and flew back downstairs.

'Stan, we'll have to go in your car,' I remembered. 'I'm too drunk to drive and we might meet the Old Bill. Oh, sorry, that's you!'

He laughed. 'You're a bugger you are. All right, but don't let that smelly old sheepdog get on the seats or my sergeant'll be after me.'

By the time we caught up with the sheep they had covered quite a distance and it became apparent that it was going to be no easy matter getting them home. They were enjoying their freedom and the delicious taste of the roadside grass seemed to be preferable to that in the field.

As we drove up behind them Stan said, 'What d'you want me to do? Stop here?'

'No, go right through them and then turn around so we can drive them back in front of us,' I explained.

He eased the car gingerly through the scattering flock and then turned in a gateway.

'Right. I'll get out here,' I said, opening the door. 'Can you follow behind in case any cars come? Thanks.'

Feeling slightly light headed I wondered briefly whether there was a law against driving sheep whilst under the influence of alcohol. Still, even if there was I doubted Stan Cripps was going to do anything about it.

'Jess,' I shouted, 'come by, come by,' and gave her the command for running to my left. 'Send 'em on. Good girl. Away to me.' Now she ran to the right.

The sheep stopped abruptly, surprised to find their master and his dog out at that time of night. Panicking, as sheep do, they started streaming

67

back along the road where they had just come from.

'Jess, steady now, steady,' I yelled as the flock gathered pace and a scatty old ewe belted at full pace into a roadside ditch and disappeared.

'Hold on, Stan – where's that one gone?' I shouted as he drew alongside.

'I'll have a look, you keep up with the rest,' he offered and climbed out of the car.

After a minute I heard him shout, 'Can't get the bugger to move. You'll have to help.'

I ran back and together we pulled her out of the ditch. 'She won't stand up,' Stan pointed out. 'What's wrong with her?'

'I don't know,' I replied, trying to pull her to her feet. 'I think she must have damaged a leg.'

'What'll we do with her now?'

'We'll have to put her in your car.'

'In the car! It's a police car. I can't have a bleeding sheep in there,' he said aghast.

'Why not? She's not going to do anything.'

'It'll crap everywhere,' he said.

'No, she won't. Anyway there's nothing else we can do. I can't carry her home. Come on, we'll wedge her behind the back seat.'

With a great deal of reluctance he helped shove her on to the back seat all the while issuing dire warnings of what would happen if she misbehaved.

The rest of the flock had now disappeared around the corner so we sped off after them. Jess found it very exciting sharing a police patrol car with a sheep, Stan less so. As we rounded the bend there was no sight of them.

'Where the hell...? Oh blast, they're in Mr Tozer's garden. Damn.'

He was a miserable old bachelor who seemed to spend his whole life complaining about something or other.

'Bugger this!' I exploded, startling PC Cripps. 'How on earth are we going to get them out without waking him up?' I looked at my watch. Half past two in the morning. I had to get them out without him ever knowing or I'd never hear the end of it.

'Stan, can you leave the car here and come in and help please,' I asked. 'If I stand just behind the hedge in his garden with Jess and you creep round the back and get behind them, I'll turn them back on to the road when they appear.'

'I can see this turning into a right nightmare,' he uttered but agreed to do it nonetheless.

'And Stan, can you turn off the flashing light – it might wake old Tozer up.'

I crept into the front garden, every footstep on the gravel sounding as though I'd trodden on a bag of crisps, and crouched down behind the hedge out of sight of the road. Stan seemed to be gone for ages and I wondered what on earth he was doing when I heard a yell followed by the sound of breaking glass. A light went on in the house and Mr Tozer appeared at the front door. I kept a hand on Jess and stayed perfectly still as he came out and shouted.

'What the bloody hell's going on?'

There was absolute silence and I wondered whether Stan had heard him.

'Who's out here?' Tozer bellowed and started

walking down the drive wearing only his pyjamas. Then he saw the police car outside the gate.

'Something's going on,' I heard him mutter. 'Got the bloody fuzz 'ere, I see.'

By this time he had disappeared from my view but he was only just the other side of the hedge.

He knocked on the car window.

'You in there bobby?' he demanded.

There was no answer of course so he opened the door.

'Hello,' he shouted, whereupon the ewe wedged on the back seat let out an almighty 'baa'.

'It's a bloody sheep!'

I could sense that he was becoming confused by the unusual scenario when I heard another car approaching. It stopped behind Cripps', and Tozer's voice carried clearly through the night air.

'Another bloody police car,' he said and a car door slammed.

'Evening, sir,' a new voice said. 'Are you all right?'

'I was until you lot arrived,' he barked back. 'What you all doing 'ere at this time of night? You raiding me or something. Surrounding me with marksmen are you?'

'I'm not sure what you mean, sir,' the other voice said. 'I saw my collague's car here and stopped to see if he needed some help.'

'Well he ain't 'ere,' Tozer told him.

'He must be somewhere around,' the policeman said. 'He wouldn't just abandon his patrol car.'

'I told you he ain't 'ere but there's something

70

bloody funny going on I can tell you.'

'I can see that sir. Perhaps I could start by asking you what you're doing in the middle of the road wearing your pyjamas?'

'I bloody live 'ere.'

'Maybe you do sir but not presumably in the road. Why are you out here?'

''Cos of all this bloody carry-on. Get woken up, come out 'ere to find a police car, no copper in it just a sheep.'

'A sheep?'

'In the car.'

'Are you saying, sir, that there's a sheep in that car?' the officer queried in disbelief.

''Ere, I'll show you. You think I'm off my bleeding rocker, don't you?'

I felt that I ought to go and start explaining when suddenly the flock of sheep streamed around the corner of the house. I scurried across the lawn to turn them on to the road.

Mr Tozer let out a yell. 'There's a whole bloody lot more of the things. They've been in my bleeding garden.'

I grabbed Stan as he appeared.

'There's a bit of a commotion going on I'm afraid,' and quickly explained. 'Tozer's out in the road with one of your lot I think. I'll follow the sheep. Perhaps you could sort it out? Sorry!'

We walked out to be greeted by two very confused men, one in his pyjamas, the other in a sergeant's uniform.

'Oh, hell, it's my sergeant,' muttered Stan under his breath. I had to stay with the sheep and left him with the unenviable task of explaining

71

the circumstances.

'That was a right mess you left me in,' he said when he caught up with me.

'Stan, I'm sorry about all this. It has been really good of you to help me out. I hope you don't get any come back from your sergeant.'

'No, he'll be okay, he's not a bad bloke but I don't fancy your job seeing Tozer tomorrow. He's in a right strop!'

'Hardly surprising I suppose. Anyway we'd better get that ewe out of your car – we'll put her in the stable for tonight.'

It was difficult getting her out as she had become firmly wedged behind the back seat but to the accompaniment of the police radio crackling Bravo Charlies at intervals, we succeeded after a struggle.

'Well thanks for everything,' I said as he prepared to continue his night patrol.

'All part of the job,' he replied 'and I'll tell you one thing: it's made quite a change from carting drunks around in the back of the car!'

I took the old ewe some hay and water once he'd gone and noticed that she had a distinguishing black mark on her head. I'd know her again amongst the rest of the flock.

'I bet you're the only sheep in England that's had a ride in a police car,' I said to her as I closed the door.

I crept quietly into the house hoping that no one else had been disturbed by the nocturnal activities. Sophie was lying curled up in my bed fast asleep and I looked at her for a few moments, her long dark hair spread out over the pillows, the moonlight emphasising the stunning features of her face. I wanted to touch her, to run ray fingers over the contours of those high cheek-bones, her perfect straight nose and to kiss her sensuous lips. She was there waiting for me, naked in my bed and I wanted to feel her lithe body pressed against mine. I turned away and gazed out over the parkland in front of the house, the pale light of the moon caressing the rolling hills of Russetshire, the little kingdom that I was supposed to manage and once again knew that I was defeated. The estate and its responsibilities checked me and I crept away, leaving her to rest peacefully on her own.

## Chapter 8

Sophie, understandably, exploded in tears the next morning confused by my actions towards her. Later that same week I was confronted by yet another explosion. His lordship called in the army's bomb disposal team to blow up one of the estate vans.

TERROR BOMB BLAST SCARE ROCKS RUMSHOTT ESTATE was one headline. 'A potential terrorist threat on the life of Princess Davina's father, Earl Leghorn, shocked local residents this week.'

It was a pity because it was my fault and initially stemmed from a request by 'Bill the rabbit', as he was known, to have a new van.

There was a serious rabbit problem on the estate, which was causing untold damage to growing crops and young trees. It had got so bad that we had employed a delightful old boy, Bill Binks, to work as a full-time warrener. Every day would see him pottering about the place in his ancient mini-van carting snares, traps, guns and ferrets as he waged his war on these furry little creatures. He had spent the best part of his life fighting rabbits and it was true to say that he had come to resemble them, rather like dog owners seem to end up looking similar to their pets. Admittedly he did not have long pointed ears but he had that small, rather cute rounded face that a rabbit has, with a little wrinkled up nose and large doleful eyes. But despite or because of this, he was an excellent warrener and often at the end of the day he would drop in at the estate office and show me his day's catch. I was led to believe that a lot of pensioners in Russet benefited from his success although I had only his word for that.

It was becoming apparent that his van was beginning to fail and despite my reluctance to spend much money on a new one I realised that a replacement had to be found or Bill and his ferrets would be stranded. After a lot of searching for the right thing I contacted a local dealer who sold disused washing machine delivery vans. It was ideal for Bill because it had a very high mileage so it was cheap, and he would do very few miles just running around the estate. It was also big enough to carry all his paraphernalia. Unfortunately it arrived late on a Friday after-noon just before I was going away for the week-

74

end and so I left it parked in the car park behind the stable block. Evidently two people became aware of its presence on the Saturday – but unfortunately not at the same time. Bill saw it as he drove past and stopped to inspect it. He approved wholeheartedly and was looking forward to Monday morning when he was due to take delivery. His lordship also saw the van that day but the following morning he became suspicious as it was still there so he asked the police to investigate. The documents relating to its ownership had not yet been transferred to the estate and as they were unable to trace a legal owner they decided that something sinister was going on and alerted the army's bomb disposal squad. They raced down the motorway to Rumshott and carried out a controlled explosion on the van, leaving it with bent doors and no windows. What was left of it was hastily removed to the police compound in Russet.

On Monday I arrived early at work to find, to my dismay, that the van had gone and all that there was left was a pile of shattered glass. Of course I immediately contacted the police to report a stolen car. Typically for a large organisation, the department dealing with stolen cars was not the same one that dealt with terrorist bombs so the connection was not established. I went back outside to find Bill staring forlornly at the pile of glass muttering 'my van, my van' in the same tone that a priest chants 'dust to dust, ashes to ashes' at a funeral. He was inconsolable, no doubt envisaging more months of the mini-van and its unhelpful habit of stopping when it should not.

'I'm sure we'll get it back soon, Bill,' I said, trying to comfort him. 'I expect the police are already looking for it because they know that it belongs to Lord Leghorn.'

'I've waited so long for it,' he cried. 'I even saw it here on Saturday – it was a lovely little van, just what I wanted.'

'Well leave it to me to sort out and I'm certain we'll soon have it back.' As my voice trailed off he disappeared in the old van, ferrets peering out the back window through their wire cages. They looked as if they too were disappointed about their new car, their noses and whiskers flickering in annoyance.

His lordship was not an early riser and by the time he came over to the estate office it was eleven o'clock. Surprisingly, I still was not aware of what had happened. He came bustling in desperate to break the news to me and I listened in mounting horror while trying to think of a way to tell him my side of the story. He did look a bit alarmed at first but when I explained that it was insured he saw the funny side and broke into great guffaws of laughter.

Once I had sorted out the confusion with the police I had to deal with the press. Headlines like EARL LEGHORN, FATHER OF THE PRINCESS OF ARNHUSTEIN, ORDERS ARMY TO BLOW UP HIS CAR would not be helpful. By this time I had been at Rumshott long enough to cope with the reporters and I fed them a fudged-enough account to save his lordship's embarrassment and my skin.

Shortly after his lordship left the office I received an indecipherable telephone call from Mr Avery, the man in charge of forestry work at Weston Ferretts, the Leghorns' 2,500-acre estate near the Norfolk coast. Inherited by the family through marriage generations ago it was a very different estate to Rumshott, not only because the land types were basically sandy rather than clay, but because it was even more rural and isolated. Apart from the wide rolling landscape and flint cottages and farms there was little else there. Although I spent some time managing the let farms and cottages a lot of my work there involved restoring the woodlands which had suffered badly during the October gales of 1987.

'Is that Misseraden, ssAvery 'ere,' the phonecall began.

'Hello, Mr Avery,' I said, which would be the sole remark that I would get right in the following dialogue.

'SsAvery, Weston Ferretts,' he would continue.

'Yes, how can I help?' He was a true North Norfolk-born-and-bred local with such a broad dialect that I wondered if he had ever been outside the village. He and his team of workers carried out all the forestry work on the estate and so it meant that I dealt with him a great deal of the time while we sorted out the devastated woodlands.

'Thowt I'd talabot them trees you said you waanaplan int autum upton Opsill.'

'Ah, yes, um, I've got our planting scheme organised for this autumn at Copse Hill Farm, so I think we'd better meet at the wood and have a

77

look together,' I suggested, having got the gist of the conversation. At least when I got there we could talk properly even if he had to repeat things several times. I was not sure whether all his clients found him so difficult to understand, but if not, he must have thought I was a bit slow. In fact the longer I knew him the worse it seemed to get and it was obvious that he found me just as strange. When I thought we had managed to get a telephone conversation going he appeared to think it was finished and always cut me off without so much as a goodbye. It was all very disconcerting.

It was one of those quirks of fate that Mr Avery ever got involved with a particularly high-profile episode that unfortunately occurred on the Weston Ferretts estate. Inevitably it concerned a tree but this was not just any old tree, it was an ancient ash tree that stood in a prominent position in the centre of the village by the pond.

Some new houses had been built by the pond and some of the residents started the fuss. I do not have anything against people who retire to the countryside and I hope that they enjoy their last years in peace, but there were a few in Norfolk who I would quite cheerfully have suggested moved back to Birmingham from where, I believe, they originated. For a year or two these people had lived happily in Weston Ferretts until they noticed a few twigs had fallen off the wonderful old ash tree on to their cars. For some inexplicable reason they developed an irrational fear that the tree was dying and would suddenly fall over and kill them as though its final purpose in life was to land on an old age pensioner. Unbeknown to me they called in some unscrupulous tree surgeon to report on its condition. Seeing a potential job he declared it dangerous and said it ought to be cut down. The people from the new houses told the council and a notice was served on the estate insisting that the dangerous tree be felled.

Meanwhile the pro-tree lobby heard about this and set up a rival position with other experts drafted in to confirm that the tree was safe. This all took place over a few months and both sides gradually became more heated and vociferous in their allegations. I kept George informed but he was becoming irritated by the commotion. What he actually said in the end was, 'I don't want to hear another bloody thing about it. Cut the damned thing down.' Sadly that was its death sentence. But it turned out to be a slow and drawn-out death, partly due to Mr Avery's disregard for public relations.

The first time we tried to cut it down I arrived in the village to find the tree surrounded by protesters, some standing in the pond, some sitting in the branches and inevitably the local television and radio reporters on the scene. I was well aware that local television would happily report that the Number Ten bus from Clapton to Wytchwood or wherever had had a puncture, so the drama in Weston Ferretts would merit top billing in the news. Bearing in mind that we did all we could to avoid unnecessary publicity this was a disaster.

I found Mr Avery in the middle of the commotion brandishing an extremely large chainsaw. When I finally pushed through the crowd he said something like, 'Sshud fell the fukintree ontop of theesbasards,' which I translated to mean that he thought we should fell it anyway.

Of course it was impossible and I had to call the whole thing off. The protesters had won and secretly I was delighted as I did not want to see it cut down. If it had not been for the wretched people in their newly built retirement homes the old tree would have stood for years. When I returned to Rumshott that evening George was adamant. The estate would not listen to the objectors and now that the decision had been taken to fell it, down it would come.

So a second attempt was organised. This time the police cordoned off the area and provided Mr Avery with a clear space in which to work. Inevitably there was one final drama. He had miscalculated the room he needed so unfortunately when the old tree finally fell it brought down the telephone and electricity lines, cutting off Weston Ferretts from the rest of the world. In apt retribution during their moment of glory, seeing the village on television, they couldn't switch the things on.

Again I found it difficult to understand Mr Avery's words when he saw the mangled wires amongst the boughs of the tree but for once I did not try to decipher them.

# Chapter 9

My passion for horses had led me to persuade the earl to allow the park to be used for some horse trials. I had been fortunate as the British Horse Society ruling body had, at the time, been searching for a new venue for a May event.

A year's work of planning had gone into this, mainly in the physical preparation of the course and in particular the building of the cross-country fences which encompassed a beautiful three mile circuit of the park.

George had not been wholly supportive of the idea as he had an intense dislike of horses. 'Ought to be in a can of dog food,' he invariably cried whenever we drove past one.

However, his lordship had embraced the project with enthusiasm, to the extent that he offered to host a cocktail party in the mansion house on the eve of the event. All the competitors, judges, helpers and estate staff were invited and I felt a great sense of satisfaction that at last my idea had come to fruition.

Dress was formal and I stood in the main hall with Lord and Lady Leghorn, George, the High Sheriff of Russetshire and a retired colonel who was somebody important in the horse world. The High Sheriff wore a flamboyant ceremonial uniform but it paled into insignificance compared to her ladyship's outfit as she had, for some bizarre reason, dressed rather like a jockey. She disliked any sort of animal so hadn't been entirely helpful during the planning of the event, referring to it as a pony show, but had obviously decided to embrace the party with fervour.

'Darling,' she said to me as we greeted guests coming through the hall, 'aren't these people just divine?' It sounded as though she had discovered a new subspecies of *Homo sapiens*.

'Well, yes, my lady,' I replied, not sure quite what else to say.

'And I thought these horsy people were always so vulgar,' she continued. 'You know, terrible language and dirty fingernails.'

His lordship, chatting amicably, was much more at ease. He had an immediate affinity for country people which her ladyship did not share. She often said that she couldn't understand how people lived in the country, pronouncing the word as though it was an obscenity. She was attracted to the glamour of cities like a moth to light and if it hadn't been for the grandeur of the house I doubt that she would have stayed there at all.

'Oh, Sophie, darling,' she cried. 'How absolutely sweet you look, dear. What a pretty little frock you're wearing.'

I looked at Sophie and caught her eye.

'Thank you, Lady Leghorn,' she replied, trying not to grimace.

She didn't look sweet, I thought. She looked absolutely stunning, sophisticated, sexy and was the most beautiful girl to have walked through the hall that evening. How I wished she wouldn't dress like that when it was already hard enough sticking to my resolve not to get involved with her.

We had half managed to work things out between us after the disastrous night at Harbottle. Sophie had been devastated the next morning and had left early almost unable to hold back her tears. I knew I'd hurt her deeply and couldn't blame her for walking out without speaking to me. It was worse than just feeling what a bastard I'd been because underneath I knew I wanted her, more so than anyone else I'd ever met. I spent so much time thinking about her or being with her in the office it felt as though I was torturing myself. It must have been doubly bad for her as she wasn't the one saying stop.

The whole business plagued me incessantly. I knew she was right for me but I could not get over the ridiculous notion that working together should prevent us getting together. I only had to remind myself of the last girl I'd gone out with to realise I was missing an ideal opportunity. Sophie didn't complain that wearing wellies was like having a couple of condoms on your feet or that the smell of sheep muck in the yard reminded her of some unpronounceable place in Afghanistan. Sophie understood.

After everyone had arrived I wandered into the state rooms talking to various people whom I knew. Many of them asked about the paintings that adorned the walls – a breathtaking display of masterpieces by some of the most sought-after artists in the world. Rembrandts, Gainsboroughs, Van Dycks and Canalettos seemed to fill all the available space. The Marble Hall, the Great Hall, the library and the Yellow Drawing Room and all the state rooms on the West Front including the Gainsborough Room and the Chinese Drawing Room were full of people sipping champagne and looking in awe at the surroundings.

I caught a glimpse of Sophie, her tall elegant figure circulating amongst the guests. Strictly speaking she was on duty, as I was, assisting the Leghorns as hosts of the party. I wanted to go over and say how wonderful I thought she looked but she kept disappearing in the crowd of three hundred guests.

I was deeply engaged in conversation with a large masculine-looking woman who turned out to be a dressage judge when I spotted Sophie quite clearly. My heart leapt as I saw that she was chatting intensely with an extremely good-looking young man whom I recognised as a well-known international rider. I could see, because I knew her so well, from her eyes and her body language that she was flirting with him and a surge of jealousy went through me. I found it hard to concentrate on the large lady.

'A good seat's the most important thing,' she was saying. 'Keep your bottom in the saddle, holds your mount steady you know.'

I was certain that her bottom would keep any mount steady and pitied her poor husband.

'Yes, I'm sure you're right,' I said neutrally, wanting to break away and speak to Sophie.

'Of course,' she continued, 'it's in the hands too. Must have that firm but gentle touch with the hands or you'll never get anywhere.'

I was beginning to think that I wouldn't get anywhere as her braying voice offered me yet more unsolicited advice.

'Many a test's been ruined by bowel control,' she added, touching me on the arm with a knowledgeable grip, 'or lack of it I should say.'

'Shit,' I said aloud without thinking – Sophie seemed to be disappearing out of the room with that bloke.

Dressage-horse face stood back in alarm.

'Well,' she said, shocked. 'That's a rather crude way of putting it but of course you're absolutely right.'

I momentarily lost the thread of what she was saying. Then I remembered – bowel control. Did she mean the horses or the riders?

'Yes, let 'em have a good stale in the collecting ring beforehand,' she explained. Ah – she meant the horses. 'Terrible way to lose marks otherwise.'

I was getting in a bit of a panic, especially as a friend of dressage lady, sporting a lipstick which she'd rather curiously also applied to her upper teeth, sidled alongside and tried to engage me in a discussion about cod liver oil.

'You see, Marjorie,' she said 'it has wonderful properties. Helps keep their joints supple and of course it aids their digestive systems.'

Back to bowel movements, I thought. Making my own movement I left them to their fascinating subject. I smiled and nodded at other people as I frantically searched for Sophie. I hadn't realised that I would feel like this – the situation of seeing her with another man had never cropped up before and I was dismayed at myself. I had a desperate urge to find her and say something before it was too late and then I spotted her in a corner of the room sitting at a table with the rider. What a bastard I thought, coming here, to my horse trials and then trying to pick up my girlfriend. Only of course she wasn't. I had made that clear to her time and time again. I started moving through the crowd towards them when Lady Leghorn stopped me.

'James, darling,' she said, her eyes sparkling like the diamonds that dangled from her ears, 'isn't this the most wonderful party? All these lovely people here and having such a good time.'

'It is,' I agreed, 'and of course it's extremely kind of you and his lordship to host it,' I added.

'I know, I know,' she said, 'although his lordship is feeling just a little tired at the moment. You know how he gets at these things. He's resting in his study and wonders whether you could pop along and see him for a minute, something to do with tomorrow's prize-giving.'

She led me through the room, gliding regally, expecting and receiving the crowds to part before her like Moses had the Red Sea.

'Darling,' she said, knocking on the study door, 'it's James here to see you.'

'Ah, come in,' his lordship mumbled.

'Are you feeling a little better, darling? It is such a scrum out there I know. Perfectly dreadful, you poor dear.'

'I'm f-fine now thank you. B-bit tired, that's all.'

'His lordship does find these parties quite

86

gruelling, don't you, your lordship,' she started, 'but here's James so I'll go back and see the guests.'

'D-do sit d-down,' he offered. 'I just wanted a word about the prize-giving.'

'Well that is all arranged for tomorrow afternoon at four o'clock, my lord,' I reminded him.

'Yes, I know,' he said. 'I was w-wondering whether t-to let my w-wife do it instead. She's s-suddenly got very keen on the idea.'

That was not surprising. She wanted to be in the limelight and now that she realised it wasn't just a little pony show but involved international and Olympic riders she wanted a slice of the glory.

'Well, my lord, I would prefer it if you presented the prizes, particularly as that is what is stated in the programmes.'

'Oh.' I could see he was under some pressure.

'Perhaps you and her ladyship could present them together,' I suggested.

He sat up. 'Yes, that's an excellent idea. That's what we'll do then. Together.'

Having successfully sidestepped her ladyship's intentions I temporarily forgot my own troubles but as I walked back along the private passage I saw, to my horror, Sophie leaving the party with her rider friend.

I stood stock still in disbelief. My insides churned with an awful feeling of nausea. Where were they going? What were they doing? There was nothing I could do now. I was too late.

The last thirty minutes of the party seemed to last for ever. All I wanted to do was go home but what to do I didn't know. I just couldn't bear the thought of her with someone else and to make it worse I knew that there was no one to blame but myself.

## Chapter 10

We had welcomed the media coverage publicising the horse trials but as a norm the Leghorns disliked press intrusion and even favourable reports were treated with caution. Viscount Rumshott loathed it more than anyone else. He was still a teenager when his sister, Lady Davina, had married the Prince of Arnhustein and at a young age he was suddenly thrust into the limelight of the world's newspapers. Having his student exploits exposed in the news grated deeply with his sense of privacy and freedom. He tended to keep a low profile at Rumshott although his interest in the estate was obvious and welcomed. As heir he made sure that he learnt about the management, the tenants and the staff and most importantly he secured a base at the Folly which he considered his home.

He was at a distinct disadvantage when it came to estate matters because he disliked his step-mother intensely and he saw George as her agent rather than his father's. His relationship with his father was fine but he knew Lord Leghorn could be easily influenced by her ladyship. It was this distrust of most of those around him that led him to form a small network of spies among the staff and tenants who loyally fed him information about situations where he might otherwise have been kept in ignorance.

I was aware who was on his side, so as I threaded my way through the complexities of estate and family life I generally knew how to react in a given circumstance.

Viscount Rumshott's closest stooge for a long time was Dick Gribble, the head gamekeeper. He was a dangerous man, tall, powerfully built and with a fearsome temper. Typically for a keeper he stopped at nothing to get his own way. His final recourse was to go to Viscount Rumshott and often he would threaten to do so if he felt he was not getting what he wanted. Often the head keeper is the servant on the closest terms with the owner particularly if the shoot is the owner's passion. The keeper would be at his side on shoot days and many a story and flask of whisky would be shared between them.

Lord Leghorn had a distant relationship with Dick Gribble as he was not that interested in the shoot although he had been as a younger man. So Edward Rumshott was able to build on the owner–keeper relationship and Dick became his greatest ally.

However, as the earl did not pay much attention to the details of the shooting arrangements and Edward was often absent from the estate for weeks on end, I was left in charge of the shoot. George had no interest in it either, so long as it didn't lose too much money. Eight thousand pheasants and five hundred ducks were reared, providing enough shooting for the family and also some days to sell.

Sold days were nothing short of a nightmare. Although the quality of the shoot was reasonable and the Rumshott name enabled us to charge good money the problem was that we never knew what our guests would be like. Mostly they were highpowered businessmen with money to burn and perfectly charming to us all at Rumshott. The snag came when one or more of them did not know how to shoot. The purpose of the etiquette associated with shooting is principally to prevent accidents. In one of the first shoots I organised we entertained a group of Swedish businessmen who were as keen on his lordship's port as they were on his pheasants. By mid-morning I was hauling eight jolly Swedes in a trailer around the estate, all quite the worse for wear. A diplomatic route had to be taken as I had a responsibility for the safety of the keepers and the beaters who drove the pheasants out of the woods and also had to ensure that these paying guests were enjoying their visit. We did eventually get the day on an even keel but it was not before I had had an awkward encounter with one of the Swedes. Having noticed that he was shooting dangerously low I stood beside him on the next drive and tactfully pointed out that he must only fire at birds that were flying high up in the sky, that there must be no chance of him hitting a person. I don't think he quite understood me at first because he took aim at a bird flying about three feet off the ground and blasted away.

I was livid and without much pretence at

civility informed him that one more shot like that and I would have to ask him to leave the party. This did get through but by way of explanation he said in a thick Swedish accent, 'At home we zhoot all at one metre high zo iz difficult me to change here.'

I was appalled, it seemed frightfully unsporting to be shooting birds so low to the ground, but he then added, 'You zee I only ever zhoot reindeer in Lapland before this day.'

Apart from this man, who obviously intended to put Father Christmas out of business, by and large our paying guests enjoyed their days and I welcomed the day out of the office looking after them.

It was a pity that the earl did not have more interest in the shoot or indeed in the estate as a whole but he was in his mid-sixties and not being in the best of health the fulfilment of being more involved must have waned. He generally confined himself to his photography and spent a lot of time with his grandchildren.

One of his lordship's greatest delights was holding the annual Christmas party for all his grandchildren. He would also invite local friends' children and went to enormous trouble to get it organised, buying presents, getting a Christmas tree decorated and having the chef prepare a wonderful tea. It must have been absolute heaven for the children who would have the run of a vast house. I did not get involved with it at all as Lord Leghorn insisted on sorting it all out himself, except for the donkey. He had found some old boy somewhere miles away who would come down to Rumshott dressed as Father Christmas and bring with him a donkey and cart. Inconveniently Father Christmas couldn't drive a car so I had to go and fetch him in the Land Rover wondering how on earth, after qualifying as a chartered surveyor, I ended up driving around Russetshire with Father Christmas and a donkey. When we got back to Rumshott all the presents were piled into the cart and the donkey was ushered into the huge marble-floored hall where the presents were handed out to the children. I am sure that any child who has ever been lucky enough to attend Lord Leghorn's Christmas party will remember it for the rest of their lives.

Every party at Rumshott was planned with meticulous care. Lord and Lady Leghorn were generous hosts and their parties were legendary. No expense was spared and many times, having been kindly invited to some celebration or other, I reeled out of the house high on a euphoric mix of sumptuous foods and champagne.

However, there was one aspect of this entertaining that caused a great deal of trouble and it was all due to the dining room table. There were two dining rooms in the house, one small one in the private wing, which the Leghorns used on a daily basis, and the state dining room. This vast ornate room was about twice the size of a tennis court and contained a table of near similar proportions. It would certainly sit fifty people with ease and was hated by the estate workmen with such venom that one mention of it and they would disappear instantly. The problem was that her ladyship was forever wanting it moved out of the house, back in again, out again and so it went on. For some events she preferred to use dozens of small round tables, rather like the ones found in marquees at weddings, and at other times she wanted the state table. At certain times of the year it seemed as though it was being moved every other day and although it could be dismantled into dozens of pieces it was a valuable antique and a great deal of care had to be taken. The men certainly developed an antipathy towards it but no amount of persuasion could encourage her ladyship to leave it where it belonged.

Rather perversely there was one memorable occasion when we were trying to move something to help the smooth running of her entertaining and she insisted everything was left in place. That was the day when Lady Leghorn took on the men of the Arnhustein Royal Flight Corps.

The lawns at the front of Rumshott House were bisected by the driveway which formed a large gravel cross about twenty feet wide and a hundred yards long. The lawns and gravel were kept in pristine condition by Hawthorne but the area looked somewhat bare until Lady Leghorn decided to place a large number of potted bay trees along the sides of the driveway. Each bay tree was about eight feet high, shaped into a ball on a long clear stem and planted in a heavy wooden box two feet square. The plants were heavy and liable to fall over so it would take two men and a fork-lift tractor to move each one. Normally they stayed outside all summer until the onset of the frosts when Hawthorne would, with the help of Tim Georgeson, the head forester, move them inside.

On the day in question, Princess Davina was due to make an official visit to Russet. It had been arranged that the royal helicopter would land at Rumshott where she could have a private lunch beforehand with her father and stepmother. The procedure even for such a minor event was pretty complicated. The day before HRH was due to arrive there was a massive security check carried out in the vicinity of the house and park which meant that a lot of sniffer dogs, policemen and surveillance equipment suddenly descended on the estate, causing utter chaos. It threw the estate office into disarray because the people responsible for the royal protection based themselves there. Added to an already difficult situation we had the men from the Royal Flight camping with us as well. They were in charge of the royal aircraft and were on site whenever a royal helicopter was to make a landing in order to ensure safety. The team included a doctor, a fire crew complete with fire engine and a couple of men who waved ping-pong bats at the pilot as he landed.

Part of their job was to find a suitable landing site. The Chief Flight Officer came in and asked me if they could move some of the bay trees away from the centre of the driveway nearest to where the helicopter would land. I agreed and thought no more of it until the telephone rang on my desk.

'Yes, Lou?' I asked.

'I've got her ladyship on the line for you wanting to know what's going on with the bay trees.'

She transferred the call.

'Good morning, Lady Leghorn,' I started, but

94

was cut off by her shouting down the phone, 'What are those horrible little men doing out there with my trees?'

'They're moving them out of the way of the helicopter,' I replied, quite reasonably I thought. 'If they're too near...'

'I'm not interested. Go and stop them at once.' Bang, down went the receiver.

'Sophie,' I called up the stairs, 'can you go and tell those blokes to put the bay trees back.' She went out and came back two minutes later with the Chief Flight Officer.

'Look, I'm sorry,' I said, 'but I've just had Lady Leghorn on the phone and she is adamant that the bay trees stay where they are.'

He fidgeted about a bit and then explained, 'It's completely against the rules to leave them there. The problem with these helicopters is that because of their size there is quite a downdraft when they land or take off and there is a possibility that one or more of those tree things could get sucked up into the rotors.' Or to put it bluntly, it would crash.

I picked up the phone and dialled her ladyship's private number.

'I'm not talking to you,' she shouted and slammed the receiver down again.

'Oh, dear,' I exclaimed to the airman. 'We've got a bit of a problem here. If you're sure that they've got to be moved go ahead and I'll deal with Lady Leghorn,' I said with more conviction than I felt.

The men went back out and started moving them again. The phone went and her ladyship hurled some expletives at me and hung up. I was watching the men go about their work when suddenly the vast sash window of her ladyship's bedroom was thrown open and a diminutive figure was seen leaning out shouting,

'LEAVE MY EFFING BAY TREES ALONE. WHO DO YOU THINK YOU ARE?'

The men tore back to the estate office in a real state of panic. By now the trees were scattered haphazardly over the lawn and it was obvious that her ladyship had to be confronted. The men were not going to go back outside, Lady Leghorn would not talk to me and within an hour the princess would be landing. Just as I was at my wit's end, Jocelyn, the housekeeper, appeared on the south front lawn holding what I initially thought to be a white flag. Obviously sense had prevailed and her ladyship was offering a truce. It was an understandable mistake to make, bearing in mind what followed.

Jocelyn and her white flag met me in the no-man's-land equidistant from the house and the office where we discussed the terms of a treaty. We would put almost all the trees back in position, with the exception of the four closest to the landing site and the house staff would cover the rest up by wrapping a white sheet around each one. I have no idea what good it did wrapping them up and goodness only knows what Her Royal Highness thought when she was approaching Rumshott. I am quite sure though, that it would have been the only time the princess arrived on a formal visit to be greeted by a collection of bed linen.

# Chapter 11

I didn't see her ladyship during the following week and had been rashly counting my blessings when the dark maroon Rolls-Royce stopped abruptly beside me. Lady Leghorn lowered the electric window while her chauffeur stared resolutely ahead.

'James,' she shouted at me, 'if that bloody sheep does another poo poo on the drive, I'll have all the livestock thrown out of the park.'

Her face, covered with the usual layers of make-up, glared from the leather upholstered interior of the car as the man from the council I had been talking to stood rigidly on the spot, paralysed by her presence.

'I'll get it sorted out straightaway, my lady,' I replied, knowing full well that this outburst had been on the cards.

The house was surrounded by immaculately tended lawns mowed by Hawthorne as often as he thought he could justify. It was obvious to anyone who saw him regularly that his occupation as a gardener, in his own view, extended solely to mowing lawns. Such flower borders that there were bore a dismal testimony to his preference of sitting peacefully on a vast lawnmower rather than digging out weeds. These wonderful lawns sweeping up to the house in the centre of five hundred acres of parkland were protected from the outside world by seven miles of eight-foot high wall. A beautiful park containing ancient stands of oak and many specimen trees, it was also home to the wretched sheep that were causing her ladyship some irritation. There were several hundred sheep but it was one particular old girl that was misbehaving. She had ingeniously devised a method of crossing the cattle grid in front of the house in order to chew at the grass of Hawthorne's lawn.

I was aware that her ladyship had noticed the presence of both the sheep and its poo and evidently her temper had now been brought to the boil. The whole thing was about to become, as the estate staff were apt to say, one of her ladyship's 'things'.

'This has been going on for weeks now,' she stormed. 'You're absolutely bloody useless. I don't know how you run this estate. Can't you realise how serious this is? Just think, if one of the tourists slips on some poo poo we'll be sued, sued you understand, sued, so his lordship and I won't have anything left.' And with that outrageous comment she closed the window and the Rolls purred majestically through the lodge gates.

Quite used to these outbursts I returned to the discussion I was having with the man from the council. He seemed, however, to have slightly lost the thread of what he had been saying and asked if that was 'the Countess Leghorn', the one whose photograph he often saw in the newspapers or adorning the pages of his wife's *Hello!* magazine.

I returned to the estate office feeling rather

annoyed. I was supposed to be preparing yet another list of farm rent reviews for George but I was now in the uncomfortable and familiar position of having to balance his demands against those of Lady Leghorn. I knew he would tell me to ignore this stupid business and get on with something useful like making the estate some money, but unless the sheep muck stopped appearing on the driveway my life would be intolerable.

I parked my car behind the stable block and walked through into the estate offices. These immaculate offices boasted an impressive entrance hall-cum-waiting room; a secretary's office where Lou fielded most of the daily blows from the tenants; the accountant's room in which Wendy struggled gallantly with the account ledgers and my own office. On the first floor was a large meeting room and an office for Sophie. Since my arrival, George had craftily managed to convert an isolated corner tower of the stable block into a stunning room overlooking the park, a room which was such an ordeal to find through a warren of passages that he was rarely disturbed.

I entered the hall to be greeted with a cheery grin from Tim Georgeson, the head forester, telling me that a car had crashed off the main Russet road through the park wall.

'Has the wall actually come down, Tim?' I asked, knowing that if it had then we needed to act quickly or the sheep would escape.

'Yes, the stupid bugger came right through it on the Maplethorpe bend,' he said, 'and I don't know how he didn't kill himself what with the speed he must have been motoring.'

It never failed to amaze me how it was that Tim, without exception, knew about disasters on the estate before anyone else. Not only was he supposed to be working in the woods away from it all but he was the kindest, most gentle man on the staff. It did not seem fitting that he should be the one to report the gory details. Although I did not have a queasy nature, I often had to stop him from describing some of the more juicy bits for fear that I would never be able to visit that little patch of the estate again.

'Presumably the driver's okay and somebody has called the police?' I asked hopefully.

'Oh, yeah,' he replied with enthusiasm, 'and I've got the bloke's car registration number.'

'Well can you let me have it and go and put up some temporary fencing to stop the sheep getting out, please,' I asked.

'Right ho, right ho,' he said, 'just thought you'd want to know about it,' and, handing me a scrap of paper, he departed, slamming the door behind him.

I could see the rent reviews getting further and further away.

'Sophie,' I called up the stairs, 'have you got a moment please?'

I went through into my office where at least there was a semblance of calm and order. Although the huge desk was covered in files and plans, a comfortable Chesterfield sofa and the solemn ticking of a grandfather clock gave it an air of peacefulness.

'Hi, we've got a problem with that old ewe that

100

keeps getting on to the lawn,' I explained. 'I'm afraid, Lady Leghorn has just thrown a wobbly about it so could you get Hawthorne and some-one from the farm to catch it and take it away, please.'

'Where is it now?' she asked. 'Do you know which one it is?'

'Of course I don't bloody know – there's about five hundred of the things out there. You'll have to wait until it appears again I suppose.'

'Okay, I'll see what I can do,' she replied rather unconvincingly.

'Sophie, it's important that you do sort this out – her ladyship is having one of her "things" about it.'

'Oh, God,' she said, 'all right, I'll deal with it.' She had been on the estate long enough to know that her ladyship's 'things' were to be avoided at all costs.

'And Sophie,' I added, giving her Tim George-son's piece of oilsmeared paper, 'a car's crashed through the park wall. Try and decipher Tim's writing and check the details with the police as we'll want to put in a claim for the damage.'

I sat down at my desk and reached for the first in a stack of farm rent review files. Every three years each farm on the estate was assessed for a review of its rent and detailed costings and budgets had to be prepared for individual farms. It was a considerable amount of work so George and I split it between ourselves. Inevitably the rents we proposed were considered too high by the tenants so it was vital to do our background work thoroughly. I had just started to estimate the projected profitability on a dairy cow herd when there was a knock on the door and his lordship shuffled in.

I stood up. 'Good morning, my lord,' I said.

'I'm not d-disturbing you, am I?' he asked.

'No, not at all, please come in.'

Despite yet another interruption to these blasted reviews, I enjoyed a chat with Lord Leghorn, except on the rare occasions when he had been goaded into a rage by his wife and came to take it out on us.

He was a large man, both in personality and height who always behaved with the benign nonchalance of a man at ease with his earldom and massive inherited wealth. It was unfortunate that his stroke had left him with slightly slurred speech and somewhat shuffling gait because strangers often mistook it to mean that he was not quite with it. They were wrong. He had a phenomenal memory and was well aware of current affairs on the estate and elsewhere.

'I'm v-very sorry to trouble you,' he continued, 'but I wondered if you w-would come up to M-Maplethorpe Firs with me?'

Maplethorpe Firs consisted of six hundred acres of coniferous woodland on the western edge of the estate. It was a commercial forestry area and in accordance with normal forestry practice, blocks of the woodland were felled in rotation and then replanted. We had recently applied to cut down forty acres of Scots pine, which had predictably upset a lot of people who liked to walk their dogs through the woods. The whole of the Firs was crossed with paths despite the fact that the public's access was by virtue of his lordship's unwritten permission. However, this was of no concern to the objectors.

With Lord Leghorn's high public profile such matters were forever being blown out of all proportions and the newspapers loved to pick up on them. PRINCESS DAVINA'S FATHER DESTROYS LOCAL BEAUTY SPOT was the one that sprang to mind in this particular instance.

'Yes, m'lord, of course we can go up there and have a look,' I replied. 'I'll show you the proposed felling area and you'll see what a ridiculous fuss the whole thing is.' It was rare for his lordship to take an interest in the practical side of running the estate so whenever he showed some enthusiasm I jumped at the chance to take him around. 'I'll go and get the Land Rover,' I suggested.

'No, no, I'll drive,' he said. 'My car's just outside the d-door.'

'Oh, um, don't you think we'd be better off in the Land Rover, my lord, after all they are pretty rough tracks up on the Firs you know.' Not only that, I thought to myself, but his lordship rarely drove and I didn't want to be party to any mishaps.

'N-not at all,' he replied, 'here we are, j-jump in.'

He had parked his dark green Daimler outside the office door and I settled down uneasily on the plush leather seat whilst he fumbled around with the controls. The 4.2 litre engine purred powerfully as we motored off through the park at a stately 20 mph, his lordship concentrating on the driving. Whilst I realised that he owned a substantial part of Russetshire, I was somewhat alarmed that he seemed to consider his ownership extended to the main road outside the lodge gates. He pulled out in front of a fast-moving lorry travelling in the direction of Russet, which resulted in a confusion of horn blowing and some strong words from the earl. However, we soon reached a cruising speed of 30 mph and the lorry, its bumper practically rammed up the back of the Daimler, together with all the Russet-bound traffic trailed slowly behind us. His lordship seemed oblivious to the situation.

But once we reached the Firs it soon became apparent that his off-road driving capabilities were exceptional and like a small boy playing with a new toy we toured acres of the woodlands. Towards the end of our trip he turned off the main track on to what appeared to be an overgrown footpath.

'Don't you think this might be a bit narrow, m'lord?' I pointed out helpfully.

'N-no, we'll get through here all right,' he confidently assured me, as brambles and overhanging branches scraped down the sides of the car. His lordship was enjoying this adventure enormously and bellowed with laughter when we disturbed a half-clothed couple who stared with disbelief as a highly polished Daimler plunged through the undergrowth.

Lord Leghorn's infectious laugh began as a low rumble and then developed into a great guffaw of laughter. 'I've often s-said,' he chuckled, 'that half the population of Russet was conceived in

Maplethorpe Firs!'

The track seemed to be getting even narrower and I doubted that we would be able to reverse out again. I had this awful feeling that it might run into a dead end and his lordship must have been thinking the same thing because he was beginning to wince whenever a particularly loud scraping noise could be heard from the side of the car. But we continued to make some progress and suddenly a clearing on the main track appeared in front of us. With relief the earl enthusiastically depressed the accelerator, sadly just as the passenger wing mirror got caught by an overhanging branch.

With a sickening thud both the wing mirror and the branch were ripped from their sockets and crashed to the ground.

'Bugger,' he exclaimed and we returned to the estate office in silence. As I climbed out of the car he leant over and said, 'You must g-go ahead with the felling you know. Whatever the b-bloody papers say we've got to manage the woods properly.'

## Chapter 12

A million pounds is a lot of money to spend just because you don't like the smell of curry.

The curry business turned out to be one of the more expensive fiascos, which was all the more surprising because it had started off innocently enough when his lordship called into the estate office one morning.

'Hello, m'lord,' I said, turning round as he came through the door.

'Morning, James, m-morning,' he replied. 'Miserable weather again t-today I'm afraid.' He was wearing a rather strange-looking hat, his soaking wet beige mackintosh, and somewhat inappropriately, a pair of well-worn carpet slippers.

'Hello, Louise,' he waved in the direction of the typist's chair. 'Shall we g-go into your room?' he suggested. 'I've g-got to go to London later and I n-need you to s-sort something out for me.'

I followed him through into my office and closed the door.

'What can I do for you, m'lord?' I asked.

'D-do you like c-curry?'

Somewhat surprised by the question I replied, 'Um well, occasionally I suppose, my lord. As long as it's not too hot. I usually have a chicken korma if anything.' I wondered where this was taking us.

'New people moved into the flat below ours in G-Grosvenor Street.'

'Oh?' It was not like him to be unfriendly.

'Bloody place always s-smells of curry now-adays.' And with that he departed, leaving me with the distinct feeling that this was unfinished business.

I had no time to reflect on this because no sooner had his lordship closed the door than there was a loud explosion outside my window, followed by a cloud of thick blue smoke, through which Dick Edwards' beaming face gradually appeared. He was our odd job man and had been summoned, he informed me as I leant out of the window to see what was happening, by George to fix a leaking heating pipe in his office.

It was just as well that her ladyship wasn't around to see Dick's van in the courtyard in full view of her tourists as she was very particular in presenting an immaculate front to them. It was beyond imagination how he ever got around the place in his van, which must have started life some time ago as a Ford Transit. There was little evidence of the initial vehicle before me now. He had sprayed it a hideous yellow but more interestingly its existence appeared to rely on the lengths of baler twine, masking tape and strips of oily cloth holding it together.

It was a month or so later, when I was attending an estate party in the house, that her ladyship mentioned the need for a million pounds to finance a new London house. Then I remembered the curry.

When her ladyship embarked on a scheme it tended to proceed at a ferocious pace and I had no doubt that she was behind the move to a grander London home. Just a whiff of his lordship's inclination to move, in this case the whiff of curry, had been enough to give her the green light on the project.

Even for a family as wealthy as the Leghorns this was a lot of money to find quickly. Most of their wealth was tied up in assets so, as usual, Lady Leghorn managed to throw the estate office into a panic. The easiest way we could find this sort of money was to sell some of Lord Leghorn's assets to the trustees. Once again her ladyship had made our carefully prepared budgets redundant. The drama resulted in George and I rushing down to London in order to attend a hastily arranged trustees' meeting with the family's lawyers. We left early in the morning and I settled into a semi-doze, engulfed by the car's deep leather seats and the quiet purr of its powerful engine as it ate up the miles on the south-bound carriageway of the motorway. With a jolt I was suddenly roused by George shouting, 'Good God, how on earth did she get in there?' I looked up to see an incredibly large lady wedged into the driving seat of a tiny blue mini. George seemed to find this of great interest as we hovered dangerously close on her offside for quite some while before pulling away.

Having left the large lady in her blue mini, we sped on towards London. I was fully awake then and became conscious of the speed at which we were travelling. It wasn't that he simply drove fast, he drove extremely fast with no evidence that he was aware of other people using the roads and the alarming conviction that in any case they would get out of his way. Matters degenerated when we reached the city and I was able to take part in an unusual method of negotiating roundabouts. Approaching them at great speed, both of us with feet jammed against the floor, though for entirely different reasons, George would manoeuvre the car in such a way that we arrived at the junction slewed sideways on.

His unorthodox style had some drawbacks, the

evidence of which lay in the various dents and scratches on the bodywork.

Furthermore, the permanent cloud of dense blue smoke clinging to the rear of the vehicle would have alerted most drivers to the possibility that the engine was being pushed to its limits but George seemed oblivious to its presence.

It wasn't very often that we travelled together, which I felt may have had something to do with the very first time we had journeyed together, to the Weston Ferretts estate in Norfolk.

The trustees' meeting produced the required results insofar as Lady Leghorn was concerned and with George's exuberance at the outcome I feared an even more enthusiastic drive home. Taking a cowardly approach, I made some hasty arrangements and stayed behind in London to meet a friend for dinner.

I returned to Rumshott the following morning. I had not been in the office long when my heart began to sink. Lou told me she was putting through a call from Mrs Turner-White, with whom I had had plenty of previous dealings, all of which had ended in acrimony. She was, as George put it, 'One of those sorts that drives a Porsche but can't do joined-up writing.'

Over the years pieces of land had been sold for the purposes of building new houses. These plots tended to be on the edge of villages but in an effort to maintain the character of the area the land was sold subject to restrictive controls established by the estate office. It was a very powerful control and extended to every little detail such as window types, roof pitches, building materials and even the prohibition of certain types of hedges.

The great benefit to everyone was that the villages remained unspoilt and attractive places to live and consequently the value of properties in the area was high. The problem that then arose was that sparks would fly when wealthy new residents found themselves hamstrung by the restrictions. Predominantly these new residents were urbanites whose tastes were out of keeping with the countryside and, inevitably, this led to conflicts of interest.

Mrs Turner-White came from this category and she had previously encountered George's wrath when she erected, without consent, a pair of wrought-iron gates that made the ones to Rumshott Park look insignificant. She then proceeded to place a pair of concrete lions on each gatepost. Referring to a letter I found in the file I read that George had described the work as 'a rather startling scene for the small village of Church Piddlington ... a cross between Admiralty Arch and Buckingham Palace.' They fought vigorously over the lions and it was not until they met on the steps of the law court that Mrs Turner-White finally relented and had them removed.

With this history of conflict I was under no illusion that any scheme of hers would be straightforward.

'Good morning, Mrs Turner-White, James. Aden here,' I said apprehensively.

'Oh, hello, Mr Aden,' she enthused. 'How are you?'

'Fine, thank you, and you?'

'I'm in extremely good health, thank you,' she said 'and so enjoying this wonderful weather. I'm using my new pool every day at the moment.'

Her swimming pool had been at the centre of a previous saga when her contractors had dumped all the waste soil in to a land-drainage ditch in an adjoining field belonging to the estate.

It's possible that Mrs Turner-White was a perfectly reasonable person and that it was merely coincidence that her contact with us was always abrasive. George tended to judge on appearances and she did come over as rather flashy in a contrived sort of way. I could picture her as we spoke on the phone – a woman of generous proportions, especially in the chest area, very tanned skin achieved by spending time lying in a box with a lot of bright lights in the lid, and blonde hair that owed something to the contents of a bottle.

'Mr Aden,' she continued, 'I thought it would be so perfect to put up a little dovecote on the lawn. I'm intending to get Fred a pair of fan-tailed doves for his fiftieth birthday.'

I could not imagine Fred Turner-White wanting a pair of fantailed doves for his fiftieth or indeed any other birthday. But that wasn't my concern.

'Presumably you mean a little white box on a stick?' I asked.

'Well it's a bit more than that,' she replied haughtily, 'but I suppose basically that's right.'

Wary of past dealings with her I asked for proper drawings to be sent to the office for approval lest we ended up with another abhorrence gracing the village of Church Piddlington. Her call reminded me that I needed to visit one of the estate cottages in the village where the tenant, Mrs Ferguson, had complained that the old yew tree in the garden of her Victorian cottage was so overgrown she could hardly walk up the front path. Mrs Ferguson was something of an oddity on the estate in that she was an extremely attractive raven-haired divorcée in her early thirties.

Most of the cottages were occupied by families, young couples or pensioners so inevitably she was the source of much attention. The number of men alleged to have passed through the heavy Gothic front door was legendary and some said that more went in than came out. Of course this was just idle gossip and I didn't believe a word of it, but nonetheless I thought it would be useful to take Sophie with me for another opinion on the yew tree.

'You'll have to drive, Sophie. My car's being serviced.'

'Okay, hold on and I'll come round and pick you up.'

A moment later a filthy battered mini drew up outside the office door. She was a notoriously inept driver and I was thankful that we weren't going very far. I laughed as I climbed into the passenger seat and saw the words 'Lady Leghorn sat here 6 November' inscribed with marker pen on the upholstery.

There had been a crisis that day when her ladyship, due to attend a lunch in a neighbouring village, had forgotten to warn Barry, the chauffeur, who as a result was nowhere to be found. In desperation the countess had commandeered the first car available. For someone used to riding in the back of a chauffeur-driven Rolls-Royce, the interior of a crisp-packet strewn old mini must have come as a shock.

We proceeded to Church Piddlington safely and called at Mrs Ferguson's front door. We had to fight through the dense foliage of the yew tree to get there and it was immediately obvious that some remedial tree surgery was necessary. Some skill would be needed to carefully trim it back without spoiling its magnificent shape but the head forester was sensitive to that kind of work.

Fortunately, Mrs Ferguson was at home and she invited us through into the sitting room. I was glad of Sophie's presence because as I tried to explain what I thought we would do with the tree, the raven-haired beauty stared intently at me whilst caressing her shapely legs with her long sensuous fingers. I found this offputting and embarrassed myself twice by referring to shapely limbs when I meant to talk about shaping limbs of the tree. Sophie enjoyed my discomfort which was heightened when Mrs Ferguson invited us to take a look around the house. She had, she said, recently decorated the whole place.

With images of her alleged conquests in my mind as we climbed the stairs I nearly cracked when I saw the red flock wallpaper reminiscent of a tart's boudoir lining her bedroom. It was only due to Sophie's composure that we made it back to the car.

A lot of time in a resident agent's life is spent

on trivial matters that conceal an almost limitless variety of problems. Often I would get asked to deal with something or other that I just passed on to the relevant head of department – clerk of works for building matters, head forester for tree problems, the head keeper and so on. Sometimes Sophie would go and deal with it but often I would go myself as it made a welcome break from sitting in the office surrounded by paperwork and the constant ringing of the telephone.

Mrs Ferguson was not a good example of a welcome break and others could be much more enjoyable. One morning we received a call from a member of the public telling us that a footpath in Bassett Woods was blocked by a fallen tree, so being given a good excuse to leave the office, I went out to investigate. The temptation to spend a glorious summer afternoon in the Russetshire countryside was too great an opportunity to miss. I saddled Grehan and set off.

My ride took me across a large tract of land belonging to the Leghorn family over which I had the freedom to go where I pleased, free to roam away from bridlepaths. It was an enviable position and for me one of the greatest perks of the job. Once Grehan had relaxed, I let her have her head and we cantered across a recently mown hayfield to the top of a hill overlooking the valley. My house was then only a small dot in the distance, a square redbrick block surrounded by expanses of green and golden fields. The hay and silage had been cut and gathered in to the barns, the wheats and barleys were beginning to ripen. The heady scent of summer filled my nostrils as we took a course avoiding the villages towards the crest of a massive drop that ran along the edge of the hill above Melton and the western part of Russetshire.

The area immediately around Rumshott had a delightful mixture of arable, dairy and sheep farms. The livestock farms with their grassy fields were superb for riding and as we skirted Little Bassett we encountered several flocks of sheep with their half-grown lambs and a herd of cattle which pranced alongside us as we cantered through. Heading for the Spire at the Bassett crossroads we trotted across the main road and wound our way down a steep narrow track to the bottom of the escarpment. Once we were on the level pastures of the valley bottom I galloped Grehan towards the woods where I had to find the fallen tree. The sense of freedom was absolute. The warmth of the sun, the rushing air and the smell of a horse elevated me a million miles above cottage repairs and blocked lavatories.

I found the tree easily enough and made a mental note to have a word with Tim Georgeson about it. I was enjoying myself so much that I took another, longer route back through very different countryside to the ride out. We kept to woodland paths through the area around Harbottle, riding on hardly used grass tracks. Grehan would jump when an alarmed, squawking pheasant suddenly flew up in front of us out of the hedge but otherwise the woods were silent in the hot sunshine. Where the trees had grown over the paths their shade provided refreshing patches of cool air as we picked our way through the trees, eventually reaching the park boundary marked by the great stone wall that circled the seven-mile perimeter.

We followed the wall through an overgrown thicket of scrub until we found a blue wooden door set in the stonework. After searching in my pockets for the key whilst Grehan fidgeted impatiently, I was able to let ourselves through. It was like holding the secret key to Narnia, like stepping out of the back of the wardrobe into a blaze of light and wonder. We had entered the southern edge of the park, high on the hills above Rumshott itself.

Great swathes of ancient parkland swept down in front of us towards the mansion house in the far distance. Massive oak, ash and cedar trees planted hundreds of years earlier gracefully stood guardian over this inner sanctum of a privileged existence.

I rode Grehan towards Rumshott, marvelling at the vision of long passed designers, imagining how hundreds of men must have spent years of toil creating this classically beautiful English landscape. I veered off the main avenue framed by its resplendent oaks towards the oval lake in the arboretum near the house. This was a jewel amongst jewels, the enormous expanse of gently rippling waters calming the most tired of minds, a safe haven from the rigours of modern-day life. Grehan's hooves crunched on the gravel track that circumnavigated the lake and a variety of water birds skimmed across the surface, taking refuge on the island in the centre of the lake.

Continuing on through the arboretum under the canopies of dozens of different species of trees we cut up alongside the cricket pitch on the north side of the house and into the deer park. A small herd of fallow deer, startled by our appearance, floated away in front of us and stopped on a hillock to watch us disappear by the West Lodge.

From the lodge I cantered along the track through Boydell Belt, another stretch of woodland, towards the parish church of St Peter, Great Bassett. The sandstone tower standing on the highest point of the hill above the park and village could be seen for miles around. It was worth the stop for a few moments to enjoy the view before trotting back down the lane home when for a while I would leave all this behind and return to the endless ringing of the phone, the clatter of the fax and the whining of Louise's typewriter.

## Chapter 13

I had always understood that managing an estate is a professional business and a comprehensive knowledge of property law surveying and farming, amongst a host of other subjects, is essential. What I hadn't realised was how much time would be spent dealing with people and balancing one person's needs against another's. It was about trying to understand what individuals

117

want. Many things forever perplexed me. I could never understand why people would drive miles to have a picnic in the countryside only to stop at the side of the main road and have their sandwiches coated in a fine layer of exhaust fumes. I often couldn't understand why her ladyship had been roused into a rage and I never understood how Bill Binks lost a ferret in the estate office.

His ferrets were not only the tools of his trade but also the love of his life. He wore an enormous duffel coat which benefited from a great number of sagging pockets and all sorts of extraordinary items poked out of the tops: pieces of string and wire, an estate map, several carrots and on this occasion, a pale brown ferret. He had brought it in to show Louise who had never seen one before. Unfortunately, as she was stroking the animal it bit her finger. In the ensuing fracas the frightened ferret ran off and disappeared behind a filing cabinet, never to be seen again. Bill was distraught and spent the next few days lurking about the stable block trying to find it but to no avail. I implored him to keep the incident to himself as I was only too well aware of the close proximity of her ladyship's tearoom. The repercussions of its appearance alongside a chocolate gateau would have been unimaginable and I preferred that she knew nothing about it.

I became temporarily paranoid about it and when his lordship knocked on the door saying he'd got something for me, I feared that he was about to produce the ferret from his pocket.

'Morning, my lord,' I said nervously, looking anxiously for moving bulges within his overcoat.

'Hello, James, I've g-got something f-for you,' he announced, patting his pockets with what I thought was alarming nonchalance.

'Ah, here we are,' he continued, withdrawing an envelope.

A wave of relief swept over me as I took the proffered letter.

'I do h-hope you can g-go,' he said as I read the note. Enclosed were two centre court tickets for the Wimbledon Tennis Championships. 'I'm a d-debenture holder as you know and I thought perhaps you'd enjoy a day.'

'Well I'll make sure I can go my lord, thank you so much. It's really very kind of you.'

I had a temporary dither over who to take but in due course Sophie and I spent a day watching some superb tennis at Wimbledon on one of the rare times during the tournament when the sun shone from a cloudless blue sky. In honour of the occasion I took a new wicker picnic basket on its first outing. Containing plates, glasses and cutlery it had been given to me by some college friends as a housewarming present when I had moved to Rumshott but I hadn't yet found the right opportunity to use it. Wimbledon was an obvious choice and with Sophie's painstakingly prepared picnic packed carefully into a cool box we were ideally set for the day.

I felt a sense of euphoria as I luxuriated in the grand surroundings of such a prestigious event with Sophie beside me looking absolutely stunning in a short, pale blue dress that emphasised her slim body and long brown legs. It seemed as though nothing could interrupt the perfection of the day until I dropped the picnic basket and out spilled a collection of explicit sex aids – along with some plates and cutlery – on to the hallowed turf of the All England Lawn Tennis Club. My embarrassment was intense as several bystanders looked on disapprovingly and although Sophie found it hilariously funny, I made a mental note to repay those kind college friends when the chance arose.

Having spent a day watching balls being knocked back and forth over a net, it was ironic that driving into work the following morning I should witness one of his lordship's balls being knocked off the gate post by a lorry. The lodge gates to the park were constructed of heavy ornate cast iron, painted blue and topped with a pair of golden balls. Wonderfully flamboyant, they formed an impressive entrance to Rumshott.

This was typical of the sort of irritating problem that landed on my desk. Besides the copious amount of paperwork dealing with insurance claims and quotations for repairs, there was the physical task of arranging to remove the gates, which weighed several tonnes, and finding an ironworks capable of carrying out the work. On top of that her ladyship took the unreasonable view that it was the estate's fault it ever happened, presumably because the lorry was delivering building materials to the estate yard.

'Why is one of his lordship's balls lying on the ground by the East Lodge?' she demanded over the telephone. Resisting the temptation to reply that she ought to know better than me, I explained what had happened.

'Get them fixed immediately,' she said. 'We've got to be able to close the gates for security. You know how important that is, and besides I don't want my visitors to see all that mess as soon as they arrive at Rumshott.'

'Yes, Lady Leghorn,' I replied. 'I've already started sorting it out and the gates will be going off today for repairs.'

'Well from now on I am banning any lorries from coming into the park.'

'Oh.' I sighed wearily. 'That's not really feasible my lady, we have delivery lorries coming in every day, not only to the estate yard but also to the house, and of course there are all the coaches.'

'Then have them widened,' she commanded.

'We'll certainly look at that suggestion,' I replied to a dead phone. She had already cut me off.

Although Lady Leghorn pounded the estate office with relentless demands and tended to blame any mishaps on us she also possessed many admirable qualities. Her tough stance and strong character got things done, she could be generous and she had an excellent sense of humour. When we weren't in the midst of some crisis or other she would call into the office and be delightfully amusing and engaging. It didn't happen often but it was enough to remind me that underneath the imperious exterior was a person to respect. Working for her tested my skills of diplomacy severely, but before starting at Rumshott I had been warned what would be involved. My previous employer had written me a note of farewell saying, 'The best of luck in your new job, and don't let the Countess eat you for breakfast.'

My thoughts were interrupted by George pounding down the stairs and into my office.

'What the bloody hell is this?' he demanded, thrusting an invoice under my nose.

I looked at it apprehensively. Once I'd passed bills for payment he would sign the cheques but only after careful inspection.

'Ah, that's for Les Cutler's greenhouse repairs, I'm afraid.'

'We're not responsible for those – that's tenant's responsibility.'

'Well there was a bit of a disaster if you remember, when we had to cut down that tree in his garden.'

'What's that got to do with it?'

'Well somehow Tim Georgeson made a bit of a balls-up of it and half the tree went through the greenhouse. So I'm afraid we've got to pay for it.'

'If it's Tim's fault he can pay,' he retorted.

'No, not really. He warned us that it was too difficult a job for him but you wouldn't agree to paying for a tree surgeon.'

'I don't remember all this.'

'Well I do and we've really got to pay it.'

The whole episode had been a disaster from the start and in hindsight I wished I'd never had the thing cut down. Old Les Cutler had telephoned to say that large branches of the tree were falling on to the cottage whenever we had a storm and after inspecting it with Tim Georgeson we found that it was nearly dead, leaving little option but to chop it down.

It was a vast gnarled old oak, its trunk twisted

and contorted like a deformed ballet dancer, its dead limbs reaching up into the sky above the roof of the house. In its heyday it would have been a commanding presence over a corner of the village but all that remained was the skeleton of its former glory. It no longer sheltered Mr Cutler's garden but loomed menacingly above his chicken run, greenhouse and pigeon loft. There was not much room to fell it as the garden was kept in the old-fashioned manner of a true country dweller and every square inch of land was dug over and used productively with row upon row of carefully regimented flowers and vegetables.

I would not normally have been on site when this sort of work was going on as there wasn't anything useful I could do and the men were better left alone to get on with it. However, I happened to be driving through Great Bassett that morning so when I saw a group of villagers standing outside Les's gate I stopped and went in to see what was going on.

'Good morning, Les,' I said as he held the garden gate open for me. He was attired in what I always thought of as his pigeon fancier's outfit – a pair of blue dungarees, checked shirt with frayed collar and sleeves rolled halfway up his arms, enormous black steel toecapped boots and the inevitable cloth cap with a worn and greasy peak.

His ruddy face broke into a grin. 'Ah, morning t'you, Mr Aden,' he replied in as broad a Russetshire dialect as you might find. 'Come t'see t'awd girl come down, eh?'

'Well I was just passing and saw you'd got quite an audience, Les.'

'We 'ave that.'

'Tim's going to have a job dropping those limbs off in here isn't he? Not much room.'

'Naw, I like to grow a few bits for the 'ouse, ye know.'

I looked around at the mass of plants, the chickens and his racing pigeons.

'I hope all this noise isn't going to upset your pigeons,' I shouted as the chainsaw started. 'They might not come home again after your next race.'

'Nope. They'll be all right. Them's just birds,' he reassured me as there was a resounding crash from the tree and a large branch crashed through his greenhouse catching the corner of his chicken run as it fell.

I stared in dismay and an excited buzz ran through the crowd outside in the lane, their patience well rewarded. The saw stopped and I heard some distressingly unpleasant language from the heights of the tree as Tim looked down on his handiwork.

'Bugger me. That's torn it,' remarked Les with some concern in his voice. 'What the bloody 'ell you up to, Tim, boy?' he shouted up the tree.

'Sorry, Les, I'd hardly started cutting and the whole thing just snapped off.'

By this time the startled hens had escaped from the remnants of their run and were scattered over the garden. So trying to put some degree of order back into the proceedings, I suggested we catch them before they disappeared.

124

'We'd better shut them in the coop for now,' I said to Les. 'Get some of these people to help.'

The situation quickly deteriorated into a farce with half the pensionable population of Bassett stumbling about Mr Cutler's vegetables endeavouring to grab his Rhode Island Reds. I reflected that it was a good job the pigeon shed hadn't been hit, as at least these birds couldn't fly.

Once the chickens had returned to the coop and the villagers to their watching post Tim continued sawing bits off the tree. At least he now had somewhere to drop them and it was fortunate that Les's greenhouse had been nearly empty or the estate's bill would have been even larger.

I didn't recount all this to George as he stood there fiddling with the invoice and could sense that he was about to strike up another argument when the phone rang.

I picked it up instantly. 'Yes, Louise.'

'I've got Mr Smith-Williams on the line. Are you in?' Normally I would have evaded the call but with George beginning to pace around my desk like a lion about to seize its prey, I welcomed the intrusion.

Rodney Smith-Williams liked to think of himself as a flock master though quite where he got that expression from I had no idea. He was a retired army officer who worked in London as a chartered accountant and commuted daily from a farmhouse that he had bought from the estate. The house was surrounded by a small meadow and when he had first moved there he had asked my advice about keeping a few sheep. He now had four of them and I helped him dip them in my sheep dip at Harbottle every year.

'James Aden here,' I said.

'Ah, James. Are you keeping well?' he asked.

'Fine, thank you. And you?'

'Yes, I am, thank you. Now I was wondering if I could bring my sheep over to dip on Saturday. I'm having a bit of trouble with blow fly.'

'Oh. Right. Yes. Well I'll be dipping mine next week so the dip can be ready by then. What sort of time would you like to come over?'

'Say ten o'clock. Is that okay?'

'Right I'll expect you then. Will you bring any-one to help you?'

'Yes, I'll bring Kate and the boy. Does him good you know. Bit of physical work.'

I gesticulated to George that the call was going to last some time and with an annoyed shrug he strode out of my office.

Although Mr Smith-Williams had been out of the army for much longer than he had been in it, he retained the air of a commanding officer, both in his manner and in his method. He arrived punctually at ten o'clock the following Saturday driving an exceptionally old red tractor towing a small ex-army trailer carrying his sheep. It was an odd arrangement as the trailer had no roof and a large piece of netting had been thrown over the top to stop the sheep jumping out. His boy, Nicholas, stood on the back of the tractor look-ing suitably embarrassed as if in anticipation of the pantomime that was about to unfold while his wife followed hesitantly in the car.

Mr Smith-Williams' precise manner collapsed

when it came to sheep. He treated them, Nicholas and myself as though we were some of his long-gone soldiers and whilst Nicholas and I obeyed his orders, the sheep merely panicked and scattered. It didn't help that he was slightly deaf as his shouting only aggravated matters. He was a tall, impressive-looking man and it was easy to imagine that before he had taken to wearing spectacles and a hearing aid he had commanded a battalion of soldiers with absolute certainty.

The only certainty I was then assured of was that at some point over the following hour he would fall into the sheep dip. He always did.

At Harbottle we dipped a thousand sheep with a lot less confusion than Mr Smith-Williams produced with his four. The air rang blue with his cries as the unfortunate Nicholas ran around after them.

'Don't be a pansy boy, grab it,' he would shout.

'Got the bugger,' he screamed as he rugby-tackled one of the poor ewes before hurling it into the dip.

'Hold her down, boy, hold her down,' he cried, 'like this.'

The ewe was thrashing about in the water when his glasses fell off, sliding to the bottom of the tank, and as the sheep emerged unexpectedly at speed Mr Smith-Williams, making a desperate attempt to hold on to her, tumbled in head first He reappeared spluttering 'strong ewe that, strong ewe' and proceeded to organise the next. His wife, a quiet timid woman, took no part in the event except to exclaim at regular intervals,

'Rodney darling, language.'

And so I met many people, all of whom played a part in my life on the estate. For hundreds of years the land and buildings had remained more or less the same and the real challenge of the job was to humour, advise and enjoy the characters of our society.

Every variation was present in this isolated world: rich and poor, princesses and commoners, old and young, funny and sad. The variety made it what it was but there was one constant that never changed. George's obsession with shoes. No matter how hard I tried my shoes always seemed to have some evidence of country life on them and whilst I accepted it without qualm, it obviously distressed him.

'What the bloody hell's stuck to your foot?' he would say, or, 'Had a pigeon roosting on your knee?'

On the first day of every month I would arrive at the estate office to find a silver metal tin lying on my desk with a large note beside it saying 'use this'. It was a tin of shoe polish.

## Chapter 14

In common with many rural estates, some of the villages benefited from local charities set up in Victorian times, the aim of which was to aid the poor. The original funds came from wealthy local people and the income from the subsequent investments was to be distributed to villagers in need. The Maplethorpe Village Charity was the one associated with the estate and by hereditary custom the Earl Leghorn or his representative, which was me, sat as a trustee. These charities were really rather past their usefulness as the income had dwindled away after a hundred years of inflation and there was not a great deal one could do with the small amount of money now available. The charity tended to rely heavily on distributing bags of coal. They were however an interesting part of English social history and for that reason there was never any shortage of people willing to become trustees. They varied from rather grand benevolent types to working people interested in local causes.

The Maplethorpe Charity was made up of such diverse folk and chaired by the local electrician who had been born and educated in the village. He was a very dedicated man and serious about his position but he always referred to the clerk in the way it is spelt, rather than the normal way of pronouncing 'a' not 'e'.

This regularly set me off in a fit of giggles which I would then have to try and conceal from the other worthy stalwarts of the community sitting on the committee. We met four times a year in the upstairs room of the estate office where we would proceed to wade through a lengthy agenda. Our chairman was ponderously slow and obtusely, the more minor the item the longer the discussions would take. If Miss Ambrose had been given twenty pounds towards her coal bill for the coming winter then surely Mrs Elliot should have the same, since she was of similar means. But then one of the other trustees had noticed that Mrs Elliot had got a new deckchair during the summer so perhaps her need was not as great. And so it would go on. I found these meetings most frustrating as I felt the whole business could be dealt with in half an hour.

Bramble, my black Labrador puppy, evidently shared my feelings and took it upon herself to express her thoughts one particularly drawn out evening. She slunk off downstairs and left a message in the middle of our impressive reception hall. She timed it perfectly so that as the worthy villagers of Maplethorpe descended the stairs they were greeted with a large steaming brown pile to circumnavigate. Their embarrassment was intense, to the extent that I wondered if they thought I'd done it myself. Although I hastily covered it with a waste paper basket they shuffled warily past as I ushered them out of the door.

Lord Leghorn avoided local meetings and the only one he attended on a regular basis was that of the Rumshott parish council. This was not a strenuous affair for him, primarily because it only met once a year and in the dining room of Rumshott House. The meeting would last for exactly five minutes, followed by a fifteen-minute sherry break. According to the parish clerk, Frederick Albright, who had held the post for forty-six years, the routine had never altered. George and myself were the only other parish councillors and as his lordship owned the whole parish any discussion was limited in the extreme.

There was only one occasion when any matter of interest was raised. For some odd reason his lordship decided that he wanted a photographic record of Rumshott parish from the air. Quite why he never made clear but much to my surprise George wholeheartedly backed the idea. He had apparently read somewhere that poor land drainage in fields could be easily spotted from an aeroplane and so the trip was extended to include most of the estate. Typically, once George was set on a plan then it was put into practice with the utmost haste. Within the week a helicopter had been chartered for the expedition. George, having been terribly enthusiastic about this from the outset, became less so as the day grew closer and it transpired that he had never intended to go up in the helicopter himself. I deputised, going with Jim Gasgoine the farm manager.

Jim was a great hulk of a man, seriously keen on playing rugby and could usually be relied upon to join in the spirit of any adventure. He would, according to George, take a camera and photograph those areas of the home farm that showed obvious signs of poor land drainage. From this he would later be able to work out a programme of remedial work to improve the drainage and hence the crop yields.

Although Jim was of substantial stature and appeared a man of little fear it soon became apparent that he too shared George's dislike of flying. He was not at all keen to get into the helicopter and so it was particularly unfortunate that the pilot had decided to remove the passenger side door. It would be easier to take the

131

photos without it, he explained. Rarely did I see Jim's humour fail him but as we lifted off he seemed to get whiter the higher we rose. I don't believe that he took a single photograph all the time we were in the air because he was hanging on to his seat for dear life.

'I'll tilt the chopper to one side so you get a clearer view,' the pilot explained happily, not noticing Jim's face contorted with terror.

Jim was not saying much, in fact I realised he had not said anything for a while.

'I don't think he's feeling very safe,' I said, talking through the headpiece microphone. 'Perhaps we'd better level off,' I continued as the helicopter went into a steep sideways slide. I was loving it, the sense of flying free over the glorious countryside and trying to identify the various landmarks both below us and miles away in the distance. It was more difficult than I had thought because from the air the ground looked flat and familiar hills disappeared, distorting the land-scape. But flying back to Rumshott with the park laid out before us we could see every detail, identify each cottage and clump of trees and set in this corner of England stood the massive pile of Rumshott itself – no less impressive from the air than it was from the ground.

With ironic timing, no sooner had the helicopter landed, providing us with the most modern method of land drainage inspection, than I was transported back into the past by the need to join Wendy, the accountant in the office, on a rent audit. This was a monthly duty and the first Wednesday in each month she would set off in her dilapidated old car to each village hall on the estate to collect the rents from the cottage tenants. It was a rather feudal system and although many of the younger people paid by direct debit straight into the estate bank account, the older ones preferred the old-fashioned way. They would assemble in the village hall with rent books in hand and pay over their monthly rent. The halls would have been made ready and at one end opposite the door would be a table and chairs where we sat waiting for each tenant to come forward in turn. They would hand over their money, have the rent book signed by Wendy, maybe make a few comments about some repairs that they wanted carried out and then disappear. Initially I was flattered when I started going on these rent audits as the old men would shuffle about in front of the table, touching their cloth caps and muttering 'yes, sir', 'no, sir,' to whatever I said. But of course it was not me that they were deferring to, the ritual was merely a throwback to the past when the earl's agent was virtually king in the villages. People would never have dreamt of approaching the earl at the time and all matters were addressed through his lordship's agent who dealt with the problems as he saw fit. To some extent that was still the case but if somebody really had cause for complaint then they would not have hesitated to write to the present earl.

Although many of the tenants liked a quick chat at these audits, one old lady, Mrs Latimer, became a bit of a nuisance because sadly she had mistaken my polite but passing interest in her cats as a sure sign that I was as fanatical about them as she was. Early on in my days at Rum-shott I had visited her cottage to investigate what she described as a 'terrible smell coming up from the drains'. As I immediately discovered on my arrival at the cottage, there was indeed a terrible smell but it was not coming from the drains. It was coming from one of her cats, a large tortoiseshell tom with only one ear. I quite liked cats as a general rule but Mrs Latimer adored them and ever since her husband had departed (we weren't sure whether he had died or left because of the cats) her life revolved solely around her pussies, as she referred to them.

Mrs Latimer was an absolute dear, small, frail but most agile and always ready with a cup of tea and some of her home-made fruit cake. I knew she was quite lonely so whenever I visited her cottage I tried to make sure that I had a spare half hour to stay for a little chat. This of course is what started her off thinking that I was a serious cat lover and over about a year I became well acquainted with all seven cats and their eventful lives.

'My dear,' she said as I walked into the cottage, 'these drains are simply too much to bear. It's been getting steadily worse over the past week you know.'

Trying not to choke on the appalling stench I dared open my mouth to agree. 'Well it's certainly strong but I don't think it's the sewer. Look,' I said taking her outside to the manhole cover I had opened. 'There really isn't much smell here and it's not quite the same anyway.'

'Well it must be,' she exclaimed, 'there's no

other explanation.' She was an adamant old lady and it was going to be difficult to change her mind.

'There might be,' I countered. 'I notice poor Benny is all tucked up in that box in your kitchen, what's the matter with him?'

'Oh, the poor dear, you know he's been ill for two weeks now and he just sits there all day in that box. He's getting very frail.'

'Have you taken him to the vet?' I asked her.

'Yes, but he says he's just getting old, like me,' she cried pitifully. 'I don't think he'll last much longer.'

'Well, I have to be honest with you Mrs Latimer, I think he's beginning to smell. You see the smell is strongest in the kitchen where he is, and it's definitely not the drains. Perhaps you should take him back to the vet's today.'

She hesitated and I could sense that she was afraid to face the truth and accept that Benny's days were over. Maybe she had known all along where the smell was coming from but needed someone to call in and tell her. I knew that she would be devastated to lose the cat.

'Would you like me to pop him over there for you and see what the vet recommends?' I offered, not altogether looking forward, to transferring the smell to my car.

'Would you do that, would you really?' she asked gratefully. 'And if he has to be put down would you stay with him right to the end?'

And so it was that I held little Benny's paw to his dying breath and became a sort of unofficial uncle to Mrs Latimer's cats. At every rent audit she would fill me in on all the details of their exploits, much to the irritation of those waiting behind her in the queue.

I did develop a slightly irrational fear concerning old ladies and their animals because there was no doubt that this combination had led me into some rather tricky moments.

Miss Arbuthnot, an extremely well connected and formal lady in her late eighties, had been a close friend, some said mistress, of the previous earl. She was well known for her comprehensive knowledge on breeding basset hounds and had written several books on the subject. Indeed, in her younger days she had been a respected judge in the show ring. However, she now confined herself to her grace-and-favour house on the estate, reading, drinking sherry and feeding her ducks. The house she lived in was situated in a small clearing on the edge of the park next to one of the lakes. To pass the time she watched the ducks come and go, fed them scraps of bread and generally kept an eye on them. There were four white ducks on the pond – nobody knew where they had come from but they had settled permanently next door to Miss Arbuthnot. She took this as a personal compliment and I am sure that she would have protected them with her life. She adored them but with an equal passion she detested the mallards, the wild brown ducks that would descend on the pond in great numbers and disturbed her darling little white ones.

This business with the wild ducks became a bit of an obsession of hers and on several occasions I was summoned to her house to explain what the estate was going to do about having them removed. This caused conflict because we wanted the wild ones for the shoot and Dick Gribble, the keeper, did all he could to encourage them to stay. Bearing in mind that the lake belonged to his lordship there was not much that I could do for her four white ducks. She was vehemently against what she described as 'these blasted coloured down and outs' and when one spring two of her 'own' ducks hatched some ducklings that turned out a light brown colour, she telephoned the estate office in a terrible state to declare that her ducks had been raped.

Every now and then I would call on her for a chat and a glass of sweet British sherry. I don't know why it is that old ladies insist on drinking cooking sherry but I did come across quite a lot of it on my travels around the estate and it is quite disgusting. Nonetheless we would spend a comfortable hour or so together discussing basset hounds or the damned ducks and she was glad of the company.

It was after one of these visits that I inadvertently got into a situation that caused a great deal of embarrassment. As she stood in the little entrance hall saying goodbye, I heard a most unusual noise. It sounded like the faint putt-putting noise of a boat's outboard engine. I momentarily assumed that there was one out on the lake.

I looked Miss Arbuthnot straight in the eye and asked her quite distinctly, 'What on earth is that noise?' As I said the words I suddenly and most horrifyingly realised that she had been breaking wind.

There was a shocked silence which seemed to last for about an hour before I gathered my decorum and cheerfully added, 'I think it must be the ducks settling down for the night.'

## Chapter 15

'What the bloody hell does he think he's playing at?' shouted George as I explained that Tim Worley was three months behind in paying his rent.

'Well you know he lost his job and his girlfriend has just had a baby, so I imagine he's finding money a bit tight at the moment,' I reminded him. 'So if we gave him some work on the estate, perhaps he could start paying some of it off.'

'I'm not giving that layabout any more chances.' He glared at me as though it was my fault that the man was in arrears.

'I bet he smokes, drinks, drives a car and he's obviously stupid enough to get his girlfriend pregnant. So why should we help him any more than we already have?'

He had a point I admitted. Tim Worley was not the most likeable character at the best of times but I felt that he was in a particularly rough patch and if it was possible for us to help a bit we ought to try. George did not suffer fools gladly and although he had left me to deal with the matter it was typical of him to blunder in both barrels blazing and demand some action.

138

Tim Worley was a tenant on the Leghorns' Little Washbury estate in Gloucestershire. Most of the village was owned by the Leghorns and almost all the residents seemed to be related in one way or another. So evicting Mr Worley from his cottage would have repercussions throughout the community.

Before the Leghorn family had been ennobled, they had lived at Little Washbury, making their original fortune from farming sheep on the productive grasslands of Gloucestershire. When they moved to Rumshott they retained the estate and, no doubt partly because it had remained in one family's ownership for hundreds of years, it had hardly changed at all. A substantial stone manor house, occasionally used by the family, stood in the centre of the village, surrounded by 2,500 acres of land, several large farmhouses and numerous cottages. The village was unspoilt, with rows of stone and thatched cottages clustered around the manor, gracious trees lining the lanes and a tiny church standing on the edge of the village green by the duck pond. One could quite easily believe that nothing had changed for hundreds of years.

When the eviction was served on Tim Worley all hell broke loose. The village was divided into two camps, those who thought he was a layabout and wanted him gone; and those who thought that he was being treated unfairly. I had a few difficult moments in Little Washbury, thanks to Worley's departure and it reminded me that it wasn't all fun, laughs and exciting work.

It was important to look after the estate

properly not only because we were charged with conducting the family's financial affairs to the best standards, but also because so many people depended on the structure and fabric of the estates for their homes and livelihoods.

Likewise we were responsible for the fabric of the buildings, a fact which was abruptly brought home to me when Lady Leghorn noticed one evening that the ceiling in the library had developed some cracks in the plaster work. The library ceiling was a masterpiece of intricately moulded gilt and plaster beautifully crafted in the eighteenth century and adorned with exquisite French crystal chandeliers. This was not going to be a case of slapping on another coat of artex to cover the cracks.

As usual the drama started without warning and I was instantly thrown into a crisis which was to last for several months.

'Her ladyship on the line for you,' said Lou.

'Good morning, Lady Leghorn,' I answered.

'James, I want you over here straightaway, please. The library ceiling is about to fall down.' Crash, down went the receiver. End of conversation.

'I'm just going over to the house, Lou,' I shouted as I left the office.

I walked across the driveway, around the side of the house and in through the servants' entrance at the rear. There was the usual bustle of activity in the kitchens and butler's pantry, various maids and liveried footmen were dashing around and delicious smells wafted from the kitchen. There was no sign of the housekeeper.

'Has anyone seen Jocelyn?' I shouted to no one in particular.

'Try her office,' replied the chef as he hurried past with a great steaming pan of what looked like boiled underwear.

I found her at her desk quietly going through the house accounts oblivious to the surrounding commotion. As usual I marvelled at her calmness when everyone around her seemed to be in a state of chaos.

'Ah, morning, Jocelyn,' I said. 'How are you today?'

'Fine thanks,' she replied looking up. 'I guess you've come to see her ladyship about the library ceiling?'

'Yes, I have. Do you know where she is?' I asked, glancing at my watch. Half-past ten in the morning and she was probably still in bed. I was right. 'She's having her breakfast upstairs.'

'She's just rung and asked me to come straight over and see her,' I explained.

'I'll give her a ring and tell her you're here,' she said, dialling through on the internal phone.

'Go on up,' she said. 'Fenella's already with her.' Fenella Cummingham was Lady Leghorn's long-suffering secretary and one of the few people able to influence her ladyship. Accordingly she was someone I treated with a great deal of caution although we got on reasonably well and were aware enough of each other's position in the household to understand the other's predicaments.

I walked through the plush, thickly carpeted hallways to the private wing and up the wide staircase to her ladyship's bedroom. It was an overwhelming triumph of interior design, a huge ornate room decorated to the highest standards of opulence. Massive heavy red silk curtains framed the windows, the walls were covered with carved, gilt-framed masterpieces and the furniture, beautifully made and cared for, was of immense value. Sitting propped up in a four-poster bed about the size of a croquet lawn, her ladyship was dictating a letter, breakfast tray beside her. I found it uncomfortable trying to discuss matters with her whilst she was still in bed, but she had a penchant for lying there like a French empress issuing her instructions to her servants.

She was charm itself. 'Do sit down, darling,' she said, pointing at the foot of the bed. 'We've got a real problem with the library ceiling. Have you seen it?'

'No, my lady, I wanted to hear what's happened.'

She explained that she had noticed these cracks in the ceiling, while Fenella hovered about in the background taking it all in. Anything to do with the house was Lady Leghorn's domain and it was only by her invitation that the estate office was allowed to intervene. Fenella was as protective about the house as her ladyship and the normal course of affairs was that while things ran smoothly we left it well alone. Only when there was a crisis were we summoned. This meant that as we were only involved when things went wrong, it sometimes seemed as though we were the cause of the problems.

'Go and have a look would you and then send

me a written report this afternoon suggesting what we should do about it. It's very important. You do understand and don't get any of those dreadful heritage people snooping about – we'll deal with it, okay?'

She had a 'thing' about the involvement of any planning officials or architectural experts and would not allow them anywhere near the house. She had fallen foul of them previously when she had set about the grand renovation of Rumshott but because the house was listed as a Grade I building of historical importance, these people were legally entitled to know what was going on. Strictly speaking nothing could be changed without their approval, a lengthy bureaucratic business which she blithely ignored.

The ceiling was cracking and badly. It was obviously a serious problem and because of the nature of the ornate plaster work, something would have to be done quickly to avoid huge repair costs.

I went upstairs to the Long Gallery, which ran along the west front of the house above the library. The 140-foot long room contained hundreds of paintings including many of the famous Rumshott collection. The Gallery was open to the public and was an impressive sight even to connoisseurs. As I walked up and down the length of the room I could feel a springiness in the floor and I wondered whether this movement, especially when aggravated by hordes of tourists, might be the cause of the problem. I knew that there was a void of about two feet between the floor and the ceiling below but perhaps the vibration could still be somehow transmitted to the ceiling structure.

I knew we were in for some trouble sorting this one out, my mind full of the horrors of Lady Leghorn being closely involved. I went to have a word with George, who was in his tower office surrounded by stacks of paper.

'I'm afraid we've got a big problem over at the house,' I told him. 'I think you'd better come over.'

'Oh, bloody hell. Can't it wait? I'm in the middle of a report at the moment.'

'No, I've got to get back to Lady L this afternoon. I can see this becoming one of her "things" so I'd be grateful if you'd have a look with me now.'

He hurled his Mont Blanc fountain pen down on his desk and, grabbing his tweed jacket, strode out of the office.

'She's an absolute pain, that woman. Half the time we're not allowed near the place and then we've got to be there immediately. Is this serious?'

'I'm afraid I think it is, but see what you reckon.'

We looked again at the ceiling and then examined the floor of the Long Gallery.

'Get Archie to come over and lift a few floor-boards will you?' asked George.

I knew that Archie, the estate joiner was working by the swimming pool so I soon fetched him and he carefully exposed the void beneath the gallery floor but frankly there was not much that we could see.

'We'll have to get a structural engineer in to

have a look,' George announced, 'so send Lady Leghorn a short note asking for her permission to go ahead.'

And so began the long saga of the Long Gallery floor. The duly instructed engineer confirmed that it was the movement on the floor which was causing the library ceiling to crack and he was asked to prepare a plan to do whatever was necessary to sort it out.

His report was alarming to say the least. The floor would have to be completely removed, the structure strengthened by installing massive steel girders spanning the width of the room. Each floor joist would be specially fixed to these girders using a particular type of hanger to reduce any vibration between the floor and the ceiling.

It was going to be a complicated piece of engineering work with plenty of pitfalls along the way.

I was given the job of sorting it out and I have to admit that at frequent intervals while the work was being done I was woken from my sleep by violent nightmares, mostly of Lady Leghorn in various guises. As if the project was not already difficult enough, I was constrained by her ladyship announcing before we started that the work had to be finished within three months as she had an important function booked for the Gallery, and by George insisting that we use estate labour to keep the cost down. We would only use contractors where absolutely necessary. The first stage of the project was to empty the gallery of all its paintings. As the pictures were so valuable Lady Leghorn arranged to have a team of experts from London help take them down and move them into storage. Gradually they were shifted, some of them wrapped up, the rest temporarily hung along the miles of passages running the lengths of the attics. It took several days to get the place cleared and already I was counting down the weeks to the deadline.

# Chapter 16

The estate workmen were by and large a jolly bunch but they were not renowned for the speed of their work. I found them all likeable and generally we worked well together. As their manager I found that each had different aspects to his character which needed nurturing in various ways. But there was one factor that was common to every single one of them – they absolutely hated working in Rumshott House. They all found her ladyship terrifying and cowered like frightened rabbits when she entered a room, so understandably none of them wanted to work on replacing the Long Gallery floor.

Archie Pendleton was the person most able to deal with her ladyship. He would fuss terribly over silly things which made his work frustratingly slow but he was an exceptional joiner and carpenter whose work was difficult to fault. A kind man in his mid-fifties, Archie took no part in estate gossip even though he had worked most of his life at Rumshott. He was the longest-serving member of staff and accordingly became the foreman on the gallery floor project. I don't think he relished it but I needed someone whom I could trust and who could cope with her ladyship's explosions.

He was helped by Justin Foremost the estate carpenter. Justin was another good craftsman but he was more accustomed to dealing with the farm and cottage repairs than the finer work in the house. He was absolutely terrified of Lady Leghorn, to the extent that he would quiver with nerves in her presence. A quiet, reserved man with the appearance of a frightened stoat, he liked nothing better than to get on undisturbed and found the atmosphere in the house a strain.

These were the two men initially charged with carrying out the work, with some help from a contractor who would install the steel girders into the solid walls of the house. But as the project progressed, others got involved which was not that surprising given that her ladyship tended to engage as many people as possible.

So Tim the plumber came in to remove the radiators, Fred the electrician came in to disconnect the wiring, the Wills brothers came in to remove the rubbish and the foresters came in to remove the rubbish too heavy for the Wills brothers. Lady Leghorn was in her element. Practically the entire estate staff was working on her project, she had lots of people to harass and she was spending a considerable amount of money. His lordship treated the project merely as a major work of repair and he confined his interest to financial updates and taking the occasional photograph. He was present when we had to dismantle the iron railings at the front of the house in order to get a crane around to the gallery window, and he took photos as the crane lifted the great steel girders through the window on the first floor.

As with all old buildings, once we had started work other problems were uncovered. We found that we could not get the girders in place until the central-heating pipes had been re-routed, we could not re-route the pipes until the electrical wiring had been replaced, the wiring could not be replaced until the ceiling timbers of the library had been sprayed with preservative and we could not do that until the man from the preservative company had been and assured us that we would not stain the ceiling. Progress was slow and with every day passing Lady Leghorn became more vociferous, reminding me of the deadline. George was watching the costs like a hawk and as usual I was caught between them.

One evening during the course of this nightmare I called at the house to check up on the nightwatchmen. Two security guards patrolled the house during the night and to my mind they were an unusual choice for such a job. They were both elderly, one was lame while the other was half deaf. In fact the security arrangements as a whole were somewhat unusual considering the value of the contents in the house. There was no overall burglar alarm device although his lordship did have an extraordinary system involving what can best be described as a collection of cowbells.

On every ground-floor and first-floor window there were wooden shutters that could be closed from the inside of the house and every evening the housekeeper and a number of maids would go through each room closing the windows and shutters. The shutters closed with a clasp making them difficult to break through, but just in case someone did manage to do so bells were hung on each shutter. The bell would therefore ring as the intruder forced his way through but quite frankly I don't believe it made the slightest difference to security. It was rather like expecting to hear someone sneeze when standing on the opposite side of Trafalgar Square. Nonetheless the bells were put up each night and taken down again the following morning.

As I believed that I should try to understand all the jobs on the estate, I had once spent a full night on duty with one of the nightwatchmen, a man who had been in the police force all his life until taking early retirement to become a 'security officer'. The night that I spent with him was one of the most boring of my life and afterwards I did have some sympathy with them and their habit of falling asleep. It must have been a dreadfully dull job and perhaps best suited to someone who did not want to exercise their brain too vigorously. This was brought home to me when I was walking around with the poor chap one night during the Long Gallery renovation period.

We were walking past the rows of paintings temporarily relocated from the gallery to the attic passages when I noticed a small but steady squirt of water leaking out of an overhead heating pipe and spraying on to the face of a deceased Duchess of Marlborough.

I stopped in alarm.

'Wait a minute, what's this water doing running down this painting?' I exclaimed.

'Oh, yeah,' he said, oblivious to the fact that he was looking at an eighteenth-century master-piece. 'I noticed that earlier but it's an oil paint-ing, isn't it?'

'What the hell's that got to do with it?' I asked incredulously.

'Well, 'cause if it'd been a water colour I'd have rung you straightaway but seeing it's oil it isn't going to wash away, is it?'

God help Rumshott, I thought, if we ever had a real crisis during the night!

Steadily the gallery work progressed but we were all under extreme pressure, even to the extent that the men were paid overtime to work on Saturdays, which was unheard of on the estate. I was harangued by Lady Leghorn and Fenella on a daily basis but there was nothing more any of us could do. In the end we finished the job on the Friday two days before the deadline.

On projects such as this where we worked under a lot of pressure it was vital to have a good relationship with the staff engaged on the job. It could be difficult to get the right rapport with the men, after all I was only in my mid-twenties and not long qualified, while they had been doing the jobs I was asking them to do since before I was born. We needed a respectful friendship between us all if the team was going to work and by and large we managed. That is not to say of course that we did not have our moments and although I might have had the last say, I did not always have the last laugh – as in the episode of the orange flash.

I had gone up to the workshop at eight o'clock on a freezing cold morning, the winds ripping across the Russetshire hills bringing little flurries of snow to settle in the hollows in the ground, to complain about the men pushing off early at the end of the day. I disliked these conflicts because for the following few days their attitude would be sullen but I could not afford to let them undermine my position. It was while I was explaining this to them and demanding to know why I had seen the Wills brothers driving into Russet when they should have been in Maplethorpe, that I realised I could smell something burning. There was a small electric fire on the workbench behind me and I assumed that some dust or wood shavings had fallen on to it so I continued with my difficult talk. The smell got worse and there seemed to be a little wisp of smoke in the air when suddenly there was an orange flash and the back of my jacket caught fire. The men soon put me out but to this day I cringe with embarrassment thinking of them all watching the deputy agent setting his coat on fire.

The indoor staff at the house were a very different group of people compared to the country people working on the estate. The erratic way in which Lady Leghorn ran the household and her frequent outrageous demands on the servants meant that she was rarely able to employ competent people at all and those that did arrive tended to leave quite soon afterwards. There were some exceptions like Fenella and Jocelyn but her people management skills were far from good. However, these two managed to cope with her temperament and without them the house would have been in chaos. Generally the staff that were employed were young people starting out in a career of domestic service who needed a first job and a good reference, but they didn't have a clue as to what the work really entailed. The turnover of staff was alarming and it was impossible to tell how many of them there were at any given time although I suppose Jocelyn or Fenella must have known. We had nothing to do with them except, of course, when something went dreadfully wrong.

Things were always going slightly wrong and this was partly caused by the arrangements Lady Leghorn had made regarding accommodation where she had separated the girls from the men. The male staff had rooms in a separate house in the stable block which meant that they could get out of Rumshott House when they were not on duty. The girls meanwhile had some converted attic rooms in the main house and although these were perfectly comfortable the girls could never feel totally off duty. As a result most of the time they could be found in the boys' cottage and what with working anti-social hours and living on an isolated estate, the inevitable used to happen. This behaviour led to an unpleasant incident when one girl, dismissed by her ladyship during a stormy row, sold her story to the newspaper.

ORGIES AT RUMSHOTT, I think it headlined, exposing the sexual activities of a number of the house staff. One could not blame them for having a good time and indeed I had noticed that some of the girls were quite pretty. Fortunately I was never tempted into this den of iniquity.

## Chapter 17

Running a house the size of Rumshott was a complicated affair. We were responsible for the structure of the building, some of the maintenance and improvement work and also dealt with the running costs like heating, electricity and insurance. Her ladyship masterminded everything else, a substantial task. Not only was the house used as their home, but tens of thousands of tourists visited each year and in addition it was available to hire for private functions. Fenella Cummingham spent a lot of time working on the business side of Rumshott as a tourist attraction.

Both Lord and Lady Leghorn would spend some time in their shop on the days they were in residence at Rumshott. The attraction from the tourists' point of view must have been to meet either the earl or the countess in person although I'm not sure that the feeling was reciprocated. I was walking through the gift shop one afternoon as her ladyship had just finished talking to some visitors when she turned to me and said, 'Oh,

God, such frightfully boring little people you know, but one has to try, darling.'

His lordship was more tolerant and much of the time he seemed to enjoy meeting people. He would sit in the courtyard of the stable block and chat to potential customers. Keen to draw people in, he loved making a sale of some Rumshott souvenir. His interest in people was obvious and generally he was most tolerant of the hundreds of visitors traipsing through his house, providing that they respected the fact that it was his home. If they did not, they could find themselves in trouble.

'What d'you think that bloke's doing on the front lawn?' asked Lou, coming into my office with a pot of coffee.

I followed her out to the hall and saw a middle-aged man wandering about on the lawn, stooping every so often to pick something up. After I had watched him for a few minutes I realised that he was picking mushrooms, those delicious wild field mushrooms that appear as if by magic in the short cropped grass every autumn. He was not doing any harm I thought and was about to turn away when the front door of the house was flung open and his lordship rushed out shouting and gesticulating. The mushroom-gatherer got quite a fright and I think he would have run off but for the fact that at that moment a car turned into the driveway cutting off his escape. I did not envy the man's position as the earl was indisputably angry.

Later his lordship came in to the office chuckling about the episode, his good mood fully restored. Having confiscated the mushrooms he had apparently enjoyed a wonderful breakfast, the chef frying them lightly in butter before serving them on toast.

'I s-saw the blighter f-from my bedroom window,' he explained to me, 'and I t-thought, how dare he steal my mushrooms!'

'Did they taste good, my lord?' I asked, amused.

He was laughing contentedly as he left the office. 'Absolutely delicious,' he said 'and even better because someone had picked them for me.'

I was wondering whether we should get Hawthorne to gather them first thing each morning when Sophie rang through.

'It's Mrs Phipps again,' she said.

'Oh, not again. What on earth's the matter now?' I asked.

'She says there's still a damp patch on the ceiling or something – apparently you've looked at it three times already.'

'Hello, Mrs Phipps,' I said, picking up the phone. 'I gather there's still a problem?'

'Mr Aden, I really wish you would sort this out properly you know. I pay my rent on time every month and I expect the estate to look after the place. It's in the tenancy agreement – I've looked and checked.' She was pretty agitated about it.

'I'll come down again this afternoon. Are you in at about two o'clock?' I asked and made the appointment.

This was a very frustrating problem, particularly as Mrs Phipps tended to go on about her legal rights as a tenant when things went wrong for her.

'Sophie,' I called up the stairs, 'do you want to come and have lunch with me and then look at

Mrs Phipps' damp patch?' It did her good to get out on the estate and see some of the more mundane aspects of the job.

She came beetling down, looking particularly attractive in some tight black trousers. Glancing coyly from under her long dark eyelashes she asked, 'Are you sure you don't want to look at Mrs Phipps' damp patch on your own?'

I sighed in mock exasperation. 'Mrs Phipps isn't my type!'

'Oh, yeah, who is?' she asked, flirting outrageously. I knew exactly what she was getting at.

We left Lou in charge of the office and sped off home in my car.

'Sophie, can you get Grehan in and take Bramble while I make some cheese on toast?' I asked, wondering whose van was in the yard behind the house. Then I remembered that I had arranged to meet Gerald Birtwhistle at half-past twelve.

'Actually, Sophie, you might have to make the lunch as well,' I added, leaping out of the car to see Mr Birtwhistle. He had brought a Gloucester Old Spot boar with him to serve my pigs. I kept two young sows in one of the brick sties behind the house and was intending to produce some piglets to fatten for the freezer.

I had been introduced to this rather odd man at Russet market one Saturday. He had been selling some of his livestock when we happened to get talking about Gloucester Old Spots, whereupon he offered to hire out his boar's services for ten pounds, which seemed a very reasonable sum considering he would bring the pig over to

Harbottle. Some weeks later I drove over to see him at his farm. He lived in an enormous old stone farmhouse near Banbury which, with some money spent on it, would have been beautiful. I knew that he didn't have a telephone connected but I was surprised to find that it had neither electricity nor running water. He lived in extreme poverty and dressed like a tramp in a collarless shirt, twill trousers held up with baler twine, a filthy old greatcoat which I suspected harboured a wide variety of vermin, and a pair of the most enormous boots that I had ever seen. I later learnt that he owned four hundred prime acres of Oxfordshire countryside and a large number of cattle and pigs. Rumour even had it that he was a multimillionaire, but he certainly did not look like one and his vehicle was in keeping with his philosophy on appearance.

'I'm sorry I'm late, Mr Birtwhistle,' I said, having completely forgotten that he was coming. 'Shall we get straight on with it then?'

'Yup,' he replied in a slow Oxfordshire drawl. 'I reckon t'awd boy knows he's on the job.' I could hear the boar crashing around in the back of his old post office van.

'Do you want to back your van up to the door and we'll let him straight out into the sty,' I suggested.

'Oh, you don't wanna worry 'bout 'im. 'E'll smell a sow on heat a mile away and that'll be that,' he said, ''e'll be straight onna her.'

I was not so sure. In my limited experience with pigs I found them to be unpredictable creatures at the best of times and if they escaped it was the

157

devil's own job to get them back. I was also aware that I only had an hour before I was due at Mrs Phipps'.

We did not have a chance to discuss this further because there was a terrible banging sound from the van and the pig suddenly appeared through the back door, buckling the insubstantial door catch on its way.

'Oh, look out,' he cried, "ere 'e comes now t'awd bugger.'

Without so much as a sniff in the direction of my pigsty, the boar tore off down the driveway, startling both Sophie and Grehan as it galloped past.

'Look at that,' commented Mr Birtwhistle without much concern. "E's gorn the wrong way.'

'I'll run down the field and try to head him off before he reaches the road,' I shouted as I sprinted after it. Bloody thing would soon be a mile away I thought.

According to Sophie, Mr Birtwhistle rolled himself a cigarette and leant against his van whilst I spent half an hour rushing around the countryside trying to catch his blasted pig. At last I managed to steer it back into the yard where Mr Birtwhistle had the wit to open the sty door in time for the pig to tear in past him.

'You see,' he said, 'I towld you 'ed be in there like a shot.'

I left him to deal with the pig mating procedure whilst Sophie and I ate some lunch. We were going to be late for our appointment with Mrs Phipps so I rang the office to relay a message. Meanwhile the boar had apparently done its job so we embarked on the tricky business of re-loading it back into Mr Birtwhistle's van. He rigged up a series of old wooden boards to guide the pig in and not having much faith now in his assurances I was certain the thing would bash through and I would have another half an hour trying to catch it. To my surprise and intense relief it did what it was supposed to and afterwards lumbered up into the van without any fuss at all. The door catch was broken so I held the doors closed while Mr Birtwhistle crawled in alongside the pig and fastened it from the inside. For one awful moment we thought he had come to grief as the pig squashed him against the side of the van. Mr Birtwhistle lay motionless on the floor for a few seconds before letting out the most frightful howl.

By then it was half-past two so, having checked that he was all right, we sped off to see the dreaded Mrs Phipps. It was a bad appointment to be late for because she had used the extra time to read her tenancy agreement again and in fact had it in her hand when we arrived.

'I'm sorry about this, Mrs Phipps. We've had a little crisis to sort out. This is my assistant Sophie, by the way.'

We went through into the kitchen. The house was an unusual one for an estate cottage, having been built in the early 1970s. Most of the cottages we dealt with were Victorian or earlier and inevitably were the source of endless problems. Being a newer house it should have been relatively trouble-free but this damp patch was exceedingly trying.

When I was at college I was taught all about the structures of buildings, remedies for defects and how to identify problems but in reality detecting causes can only be learnt by experience. I had not been able to find a single clue as to why the corner of this kitchen ceiling was so damp. It could not be rising damp as it was too high off the ground; it could not be penetrating from outside as it was adjoining the inside walls. I could not find any water or heating pipes, let alone leaking ones, but because I needed to say something, I had suggested that it was caused by condensation. I didn't think Mrs Phipps had been totally convinced the first time I had mentioned it, less so on my second and third visits and now she obviously didn't believe me at all. It was then that I saw the kettle.

'Ah,' I said with great authority, mindful of the fact that not only had I got to come up with an answer for Mrs Phipps, but I also wanted to impress Sophie with my skills as a chartered surveyor.

'That is the root of the problem,' I exclaimed, pointing at the kettle.

They both looked at me with incredulity, which I initially thought was because they could hardly believe that I was so clever to have at last found the answer. Sophie later explained that it was more a sort of amazement that anyone could be so stupid.

'You see what's happening is that constant steam is billowing up into the corner making it permanently damp, so I suggest you move the kettle towards the window and open the window

160

to let the steam out.'

Mrs Phipps was for once momentarily speechless, staring at me with a slightly boggled look in her eyes. Then she resumed her usual aggressive stance and said, 'Mr Aden, if you've just come round here to tell me to move my kettle, then think again. I'm fed up with this damp, it's ruining these new decorations and I've paid a lot of money to have this room done. The estate's lucky to have me as a tenant you know, I spend a lot on this house, I keep it spotless.'

I had to agree that it was immaculately kept but privately I did not think we were lucky to have her as a tenant.

'Well I really can't see what else it can be, Mrs Phipps. Move the kettle for one week and I'll come back and check for any difference.'

It was left like that so I was quite surprised to have her back on the phone the next morning.

'Mr Aden, I want you to come round now,' she screamed at me. 'Call yourself a surveyor, you should be ashamed of yourself. I'll be writing to his lordship about this.' The situation had obviously deteriorated during the night and she was absolutely livid.

'Sophie, I'm afraid we've got to go and see Mrs Phipps again.'

'What, now?'

'Yup, let's go. Something's happened and she's in a terrible state about it.'

'Do you really want me to come?' she asked, not relishing another encounter with the woman.

'Yes, I might need a witness in case I get attacked!'

We arrived to find the kitchen covered in dust and plaster and Mrs Phipps almost incoherent with rage.

'Just look at this bloody mess,' she screamed at me. 'Who's going to pay for all this? I'm not, you know. I'll sue the estate, you're completely incompetent you are. This is all your fault.'

Sophie, rather unhelpfully, was cowering in the doorway ready to make a quick exit if things got worse, as Mrs Phipps carried on.

'If I'd been in here when that lot came down I'd have been killed,' which was nonsense but I did not feel that it was prudent to say so just then. 'I was asleep when this terrible crash woke me and look, half the ceiling's come down.'

It was clear now, rather belatedly, what had caused the problem. With the ceiling gone I could see some pipework running between the upstairs floor joists and every now and then a little drip fell from one of the pipe joints. Bloody little pipe, I thought!

I assured Mrs Phipps that I would send some men around straightaway to start fixing the muddle, mend the leak and redecorate her kitchen.

I have been very cautious ever since about identifying the cause of a lady's damp patch.

# Chapter 18

Frankly I was terrified. His lordship had just returned from a weekend at Longleat Safari Park and had requested an urgent meeting about an idea he had had during his visit. Visions of herds of wildebeest sweeping majestically across the park filled my mind.

'I'm going to establish a herd of Large Whites,' he announced on arrival at the office.

There was a moment's ominous silence. It could have been worse, I reflected, much worse.

'You're going to do what, my lord?' I asked.

'I want to establish a herd of English White cattle,' he repeated. 'I think they'd look s-so g-graceful in the park here.'

'Oh,' I replied.

'Y-yes,' he continued with the enthusiasm of a schoolboy who had just found a penny black in his stamp collection, 'they're going to be my own s-special project. I shall even look after them myself.'

Vivid memories of some of his lordship's previous livestock enterprises flashed before me, none of which could be described as enjoyable. Memorable possibly, but not enjoyable and with a success rate verging on the brink of disaster I could not share his optimism.

'Perhaps you'd like to sit down, my lord, and tell me your plans. No doubt you'll want me to help in some way.'

'Y-yes, yes,' he went on. 'First of all I need to d-decide how many to g-get.'

One I thought was more than enough but he had more ambitious plans.

'Maybe a dozen cows and a b-bull would make a worthwhile start, and then of course I'll be able to k-keep the young h-heifers and build up my h-herd over the years.'

The first problem was that the grazing in the park was let to one of the tenant farmers and he was hardly likely to take kindly to the sudden appearance of someone else's cattle, even if they were his lordship's. There would also be a highly virile young bull and while English Whites may look pretty that wouldn't be much consolation to a farmer trying to produce beef. I pointed this out to the earl.

'W-we could fence off a b-bit for them,' he argued, 'somewhere near the house so I can k-keep an eye on t-them. I'm very k-keen to l-look after them myself you know,' he added, anticipating my next question.

'I don't mean to sound negative, my lord, but you're away for half the week in London or somewhere. Who is going to look after them then?'

His eyes shone with a glint of satisfaction.

'Hawthorne,' he shouted triumphantly.

'Hawthorne! Hawthorne,' I repeated in disbelief. Hawthorne had come unstuck looking after his sister-in-law's budgie when she went on holiday for a week. Hawthorne and livestock didn't mix. I was going to need George's skills to thwart this one.

164

'Shall we put this on the next management meeting agenda?' I suggested.

'Y-yes,' he said. 'V-very good idea. By then I should have s-some idea of p-prices and so on.'

The subject was duly raised a fortnight later but by a fortunate coincidence it was over-shadowed by an altogether more sinister problem, ironically involving Hawthorne.

Looking back on it, it was a pity that Hawthorne had ever got involved with the moles. Hawthorne was a man of either passion or indifference and with the moles it was the former. To be fair to him they were disfiguring the main object of his existence, the lawns in front of Rumshott House. But somehow he managed to get both his lordship and George caught up in his obsession. The difficulty was that once the mole business had started he would rush over to either of them whenever he saw them to give them an update, thereby constantly reminding them of the problem.

At first there were only two or three molehills to be seen on the south lawn and naively I hoped that Hawthorne could quietly get rid of them and thought nothing more about it. Whether he was using the wrong kind of bait or not I was never sure, but quite possibly he was feeding them rather than poisoning them because after a couple of weeks we appeared to have dozens of them. Not only were they on the south lawn but they had moved around the corner on to the west lawns as well.

George had noticed them by now and with his customary aggressiveness called Hawthorne into

165

the office. Hawthorne, being a quiet reserved man, was terrified of George who demanded to know exactly what was happening about the moles, how many he had caught, what traps he was using and so on. Hawthorne stood nervously in the hall wringing his hands and mumbling a few incoherent answers. I could see this was wearing a bit thin on George, who liked clear concise answers and immediate results.

'I'm not happy with the way you're tackling this problem,' he barked at the unfortunate gardener.

'Er, er, I've tried, I don't think...'

'Well I don't care what you think. It's not working and the lawns are looking a right bloody mess. I want every mole you catch to be left on the bonnet of my car so I can see what good you're doing.' And with that Hawthorne was dismissed.

This severe dressing down from the agent evidently got through because as the days went by, more and more dead moles appeared, carefully placed on the bonnet of George's car with a paw tucked under the windscreen wiper. For a while I thought things might have been brought under control and certainly the mole-hills did not appear so frequently on the lawn. But then the moles started ploughing up the cricket pitch in the park and that's when his lordship joined the fray.

Of all the things on the estate that Lord Leghorn really cared about, the cricket pitch was number one. He adored cricket and so too did Viscount Rumshott, to the extent that a couple of times a year they would form their own team and take on the local club. It was some measure of their interest in the game that their side usually included some players from the England cricket team and so the upkeep of the cricket ground at Rumshott was a high priority. When the moles started digging it up, what had previously been a battle became a war. Hawthorne was now out of his depth and he seemed to spend all day rushing about the place with traps, dead moles or some other mole-catching paraphernalia whilst the moles just carried on digging. I decided to enlist the help of 'Bill the rabbit'.

First thing every morning, Hawthorne and Bill Binks could be seen surreptitiously creeping around the gardens or the cricket pitch planning their offensive. And it began to work. Slowly the moles started to disappear, the numbers left on George's car became fewer and fewer and the subject of moles stopped being raised at every management meeting.

But no sooner had the moles moved out than the rabbits moved in. Although the rabbit infestation on the estate was a continual problem, they had never really got into the gardens and I was somewhat surprised when Hawthorne came into the office to tell me otherwise.

'Morning, Bob. What can I do for you today?' I asked him, expecting something had gone wrong with the lawnmower.

'Er – I've, er, noticed that, er, there's quite a few rabbits, er, nesting in the trees,' he said.

I stared at him for a moment. 'Sorry, but don't you mean squirrels?'

'Er, no. Them's rabbits in the cypress trees on

167

the west lawn,' he assured me.

'Rabbits don't live in trees,' I said in exasperation, 'they live underground.'

'Well,' he shrugged, annoyed that I did not believe him, 'there's rabbits in them trees.'

On the basis that he knew the difference between the two I went to have a look. There were a number of cypress trees on the west lawn with thick evergreen foliage that could theoretically house rabbits. I couldn't see any but there was certainly some evidence of their presence and I wondered how they had got into the garden, let alone up the trees.

'I'll get Bill to come and set up some traps with you,' I said 'but for goodness' sake don't put them in sight of the house.'

I saw Lord Leghorn a bit later as he walked over to the shop and warned him that we were going to set some traps in the garden.

'I expect t-they're squirrels,' he said. 'T-tell Hawthorne t-that rabbits have long pointed ears!'

The traps that Bill used to catch rabbits were perfectly legal and humane – he tempted the rabbit in with some food and then a door automatically closed behind the animal. The rabbit could then be quickly despatched. Even so it was sensible to prevent visitors to the house from seeing the tops. I could just imagine the hassle we would get from Lady Leghorn if anyone complained.

I left the pair of them to set up their traps and assumed that they would remember my clear instructions. The following morning I had an irate countess on the phone.

'What the hell are all these carrots doing all over my lawn?' she screamed.

'What carrots my lady?' Oh, no, what have those two idiots done, I wondered in alarm.

'There's hundreds of them all over the place,' she shrieked. 'Get rid of them now.'

'Lou, where's Sophie?' I asked, coming out of my office.

'She's gone up to the estate yard to see the Wills brothers, I think.'

'Right, I'll go and get her. If her ladyship rings back tell her I'm sorting out the carrots,' I explained unhelpfully and strode out the office. Bloody idiots, I thought. Surely they hadn't left traps exactly where I had told them not to, in everybody's view.

I raced up to the yard in my car, skidding to a halt on the rough stone surface beside the builder's Land Rover.

'Has anyone seen Bill Binks this morning?' I asked, knowing that he could be anywhere on the estate.

'I think we saw his van on the Piddlington road when we came in,' said one of the Wills brothers, 'That was about an hour ago I suppose.'

'Great, thanks. Sophie, can you drive over and find him? I need him back here straight away. Her ladyship's having a fit about his rabbit cages, or carrots or something. I'll be down with Bob in the gardens.'

I raced around to the back of the house to find Hawthorne wandering along the gravel path next to his potting shed carrying a dead rabbit.

'I've caught one,' he said, as though I might overlook the presence of a dead rabbit in his hand.

'Well, that's good but what the hell's going on down here?' I asked. 'Her ladyship says that there are carrots all over the lawn.'

He looked a bit sheepish and then explained, 'We've put a few bits of carrots down to lead the buggers into the traps.'

'You'd better show me.'

As we walked around the side of the house I was confronted with the sight of a series of orange lines criss-crossing the west lawn. They appeared to run from the cypress trees around such flower beds as there were and then disappear into the shrubberies on the far side of the garden.

'What the bloody hell have you done?'

'Well, er, you see, the rabbits come down from the trees, er, and follow the, er, carrots over there,' he said, pointing at the shrubberies, 'and that's where we catch them.'

'Right. What do you suppose the house visitors will think of all these carrots scattered about the place, Bob?'

'Er um, well er...'

'It doesn't matter,' I sighed. It was no good trying to explain it to him. If he had been asked to catch rabbits then that was it – everything else would go out the window.

Just then Bill and Sophie arrived.

'Bill, can't you think of something else?' I asked. 'We simply can't have these carrots here with the public about. They pay to come and see a grand stately home, not a lot of carrots. If this is the only way then I'm afraid you'll have to pick them up first thing every morning and re-lay them all again at night.'

So that was what happened and eventually the plan succeeded.

Hawthorne had been right, the rabbits had burrowed into the thick foliage of the trees and nested there.

Hawthorne's battles with the moles and rabbits had rather taken my mind off a little scheme I had hatched unbeknown to anyone else. On my potterings around the park I had discovered a collection of abandoned horse-drawn carriages. Although I found them of great interest they appeared to have been practically forgotten ever since one of his lordship's forebears had purchased his first motor car.

Dotted around various buildings in the park were a number of interesting carriages that nobody seemed to know or care about. There were eighteen different vehicles, amounting to a rare and complete collection indicative of an aristocrat's requirements before the advent of the motor car. It was rather surprising that they were still there and had not been sold years before as had happened on many other estates. The diversity of the carriages was fascinating. I found a small open carriage, a couple of two-wheeled governess traps and a sleigh in the garage at the Folly; another two-wheeled trap in a garage by the house; several park drags and a phaeton in the estate yard; and amongst the assorted types in the old coach house was the most impressive of all, the Leghorn family state coach. A huge black

171

carriage built to be drawn by either a pair or four-in-hand team of horses it was still in remarkably good condition: the coach work shiny, the earl's coronet clearly emblazoned on the doors, the silk-lined interior as extravagant as on the day it was built. This coach had not been forgotten and was an irreplaceable family heirloom but there just wasn't much call for its use any more.

In the nineteenth century it would almost certainly have been housed at the Leghorns' London residence. The detail of the work was superb – the wheel hubs were solid silver and embossed with the Leghorn crest and there were tasselled trimmings of the finest silk edging the driver's and footmen's platforms. It was an exceptional state vehicle built for a wealthy and important nobleman.

It had last been used at the wedding of one of Lord Leghorn's daughters when he had per-suaded a carriage-driving friend to lend him a pair of horses and a coachman. The carriage had been smartened up for the day and decorated with the finery appropriate for such an occasion. Unbeknown to anyone else, his lordship had decided to introduce a little humour into the proceedings of the day. Furtively he had arranged that one of his hunting tenants would interrupt the coach on its way back to the reception at Rumshott dressed as a highwayman.

This pantomime duly took place and the high-wayman galloped out of the wood towards the coach shouting 'stand and deliver' before, in a departure from the script, promptly falling off his horse as it shied away from the unusual spectacle of a coach and horses.

It seemed a shame to have all these wonderful carriages shut away unappreciated so I started to look into the cost of renovating them with the idea that eventually they could be put on display.

However, before that happened Viscount Rumshott arrived at the house one day with a request of his own which was to have far-reaching effects, and one that meant that at least one of the carriages would come out of retirement.

## Chapter 19

'Now where's his lordship gone?' queried George as we arrived in his study for a management meeting. 'I wish he'd be here when he says he's going to be, he's already changed the time twice today.'

George had little patience with 'farting around' as he put it, preferring things to be punctual and concise. Unfortunately, his lordship had been taking a more relaxed view recently and this was driving George crazy.

We walked back down the passage to find his lordship coming in with Edward.

'Good morning, everyone,' said his lordship. The two lords were beaming broadly at us so something was definitely in the air, not least an extremely attractive looking girl standing behind them.

Edward turned to her and, putting an arm

around her, said to us, 'Meet Elizabeth Living-stone, my fiancée. George Pratt. James Aden.'

We were both a bit taken aback as we had no idea that Edward had a steady girlfriend, let alone any inkling of an impending marriage.

'Congratulations, Edward, Elizabeth.' We shook hands. Elizabeth was gorgeous; there was no doubt that he had picked a pretty girl. She had long soft darkish hair; she was slim and had one of the most sensual faces I had ever seen. I had always assumed that the girl Edward would one day choose to marry would be an arrogant upper-class deb out to catch a rich aristocrat, but I was wrong. Elizabeth was kind, softly spoken, and utterly charming. I don't know what George's first impressions were but I was smitten immediately. She was a down-to-earth, stunning-looking girl.

We stood there chatting for a while and then, meeting abandoned, George and I went back to the estate office. He was, typical to form, already considering the financial implications of this latest development and before we had even reached the office he was raising questions that I was unable to answer.

'Do you know anything about her?' he asked. 'Have you ever met her before?'

'No, sorry but I've never heard of her. I didn't know Edward was seeing anyone.'

'I think it would be useful to find something out about her,' he mused, his mind working overtime. I could imagine him already worrying that she might be a gold digger after the Leghorn fortune.

The news was welcomed in the office with great excitement, the girls all desperate to know what she was like and when the wedding would be held.

'Steady on,' I said, laughing, 'we've only just been introduced. We don't know anything else at the moment.'

It was difficult to maintain the normal routine with the excitement of this news and before long the telephones started ringing and reporters arrived at the office to cover the announcement. It was amazing how quickly news travelled. The engagement of the Princess of Arnhustein's brother created a mass of press interest.

Until preparations for their wedding got under-way the estate had to continue in as normal a fashion as possible. I had spent some time considering what to do with the herd of deer that lived in the park. About a third of the parkland was kept separated from the rest in order to provide enough grazing for the Rumshott herd of several hundred dark fallow deer, resident since the house had become the Leghorn family seat and the park established. Since the fifteenth century it had been common practice for noble-men to enclose land around their houses and create parks in which to keep herds of deer. The files in the office revealed little record of anything much happening to the animals. It seemed they roamed freely, the gamekeeper gave them a bit of hay in the winter and occasionally shot a few to supply venison to the house. A few years previously some new blood lines had been introduced to try and dilute the in-breeding but sadly, only one of the new bucks had survived.

There were two reasons for concerning myself with the deer. Firstly, the park was becoming overstocked and the general health of the herd was deteriorating, and so a plan was needed to cull and manage them properly. Secondly, there was the financial aspect to consider: a herd of animals worth thirty or forty thousand pounds was wandering around doing nothing at all to produce any sort of income. The aim was to cull the herd sensibly in order to give the estate an income and increase the overall health of the animals.

We engaged the help of some experts and as a result built some deer-handling pens near the Folly. The deer were totally wild and great care was needed in handling them, especially the bucks who could seriously maim someone with their strong antlers. Gradually we developed the system and the quality of the Rumshott deer began to improve.

They were a beautiful sight as they grazed, moving as one gently across the rolling parkland in front of Rumshott House. Although they would never become much of a financial asset to the estate it was reassuring to know that deer would continue to grace the serene beauty of Rumshott for centuries to come.

At the same time as improvements were being made to the deer herd, we were carrying out some improvements to my residence, Harbottle Grange Farm, which had suffered from neglect before the estate took it back in hand. Whenever we were not too busy on the estate repairs I would send the men over to the farm to work on the renovation of the old house. Set high above the valley it had stunning views towards the Addiscombe hills and beyond towards Edge-combe. A six-bedroomed red-brick Georgian house with large sash windows facing down the valley, it was a grand building with a half-mile avenue leading down to it from the road. The land I had taken as part of the tenancy sur-rounded it on all sides, providing privacy and isolation from the rest of the estate.

I had been over to the farm one morning when the Wills brothers, who were trying to fix the gutters, had pointed out that the mains electric wires running into the house were so close to their scaffolding that there was a danger of them getting themselves electrocuted.

'Just ring up the electricity board and get them to come out and fit some temporary plastic sheaths over them, would you?' I was asked. 'They do it for nothing you know.'

When I got back to the office I had a meeting with George about the possible sale of a valuable piece of development land so I asked Sophie to sort out the wires. George must have slept badly the night before because he was in a terrible mood accusing me of spending too much time on trivial estate matters and not enough on this multi-million pound deal which would sort out the Leghorns' money problems for years to come. It was an unfair criticism and he knew it but it did not stop him all the same.

'You've got to be in the office more,' he told me.

177

'George, you know I can't possibly do the day-to-day estate management unless I'm out checking what's going on. If I don't go no one else does.' I was annoyed that he was blaming me for the delay in sorting out this development deal. If he got his own act together and worked with more efficiency I thought, looking at the mess strewn about his office, we would not be so far behind on this deal.

He grunted. 'I want those plans I asked you for by the end of today please.' He was referring to some coloured maps outlining the proposed development site. 'And don't get Sophie to do them or they'll be full of bloody mistakes.'

This really got to me, the sudden aggressiveness, instant demands which meant my day's plans and appointments all had to be rearranged. How on earth was I supposed to act professionally when I had to cope with his interference?

I stormed downstairs.

'Sophie, have you sorted out the electricity thing at Harbottle?'

'Well, sort of,' she said.

'What do you mean, sort of?' I asked her gruffly.

'They'll do it but we have to send in a deposit of ten pounds beforehand,' she explained.

'We bloody well won't,' I replied and marched into my office. I phoned the electricity board in Russet.

'Please can I speak to whoever deals with protective ducting for building site works,' I asked.

'I'll put you through to our Mr Dawson,' a girl replied.

'Barry Dawson speaking.'

'Ah, Mr Dawson. It's James Aden here at Rumshott. I gather my assistant has just had a word with you asking if you'd put up some plastic ducts on some wires at Harbottle.'

'Yes, that's right. I explained to her that you need to send in a cheque for ten pounds and a letter stating what you want done and we'll be out there in a few days' time to do it.'

'Mr Dawson, we've never paid deposits for this before and I need the work done today or tomorrow.'

'Well I'm sorry to tell you otherwise, Mr Aden, but there are no exceptions to the rule, everyone pays a deposit.'

This was ridiculous. George had not helped and I was in an angry mood and now had to contend with a little Hitler at the electricity board on about ten quid. If he wanted to be awkward then so could I.

'Why do you need a deposit, Mr Dawson?' I queried.

'Because when the builders have finished on site they never tell us to come and take the things off. If they've paid us something they don't usually forget. These builders just disappear and we don't hear from them again.'

'The Leghorns have been here for five hundred years, Mr Dawson, they are not likely to disappear next week, are they?' I retorted.

'Well, that's not the point. There is a rule and that's it.'

I was seething with anger and if he wanted an argument then he was going to get one.

'Do you realise, Mr Dawson, that the estate

179

spends something like ten thousand pounds a year on electricity? As a good customer of yours we expect a bit of assistance when we need it.'

'I really don't care how much you spend, Mr Aden, that's got nothing to do with the deposit.'

I had had enough of this.

'What's your supervisor's name please?'

'It's Donald Adams. But he'll tell you exactly the same.'

'We'll see. Can you put me through to him, please.'

There was a considerable wait whilst presumably Mr Adams was found and informed of the problem.

'Adams here, Mr Aden. I gather you have a problem paying a deposit for some sheathing work you want carried out?'

'Yes, Mr Adams. I've already explained that the estate doesn't pay deposits and I'm sure you'll appreciate that we are good customers of yours and you could sort this out for me.' I hoped at this more senior level there would be a bit of sense over this.

'Of course I can, sir, but we do need the deposit,' he repeated.

At that point my temper snapped.

'Right, Mr Adams. If that's the attitude the electricity board have towards the estate then you can arrange to have all your equipment removed off estate property. By that I mean every pole, transformer and underground wire and you no doubt realise that the estate covers about forty square miles to the east of Russet so that's a lot of poles. All wayleaves will be rescinded as of this afternoon when I will confirm my actions in writing.'

I put the phone down absolutely seething with fury at these bureaucratic idiots. I had no idea whether we could demand such action although I doubted it as the electricity company had compulsory powers covering much of their distribution network, but the point had been made. There must have been literally thousands of poles and bits and pieces of their equipment all over the estate positioned in accordance with these wayleave agreements between the landowner and the service industries. It obviously got through to Mr Adams because within ten minutes I had another phone call.

'It's a Mr Chesham on the line for you,' said Lou. 'He's the operational director for the electricity board.'

'Thanks. Hello, James Aden speaking,' I answered curtly.

'Hello, Mr Aden. My name's Chesham, one of the directors here. I gather there's been a slight misunderstanding this morning concerning a deposit.'

'I'm sure Mr Adams has explained the situation to you,' I said, 'and frankly I think it's no way to conduct business with the estate.'

'Yes, I'm sorry about all this. It's all getting a bit out of hand so I suggest I send someone down to sort out the work you want done at Harbottle right away and of course there will be no question of a deposit. We know where to find you,' he added rather nervously.

'Well thank you for that,' I replied. 'I'm glad

we've been able to sort it out amicably in the end!'

Ha, I thought, those bloody little play-by-the-rule-book men.

Having won that battle I felt much more able to colour in George's wretched development plans. I could be an arrogant bastard too!

# Chapter 20

Viscount Rumshott's wedding to Miss Elizabeth Livingstone was the society event of the year and inevitably it involved everybody on the estate. The service was to be held at St Peter's Church in Great Bassett, about a mile from Rumshott House and the church in which generations of Leghorns were buried in the family crypt.

The church was an impressive one for a small village and attached to one side of it was the Leghorn family chapel. The honey-coloured stone walls, stained glass windows and solid bell tower gave it an understated grandeur that was fitting for this important occasion. It stood on a hilltop overlooking the park and the rolling hills of Russetshire.

The wedding itself was arranged by Edward, Elizabeth and their families but a lot of the preparation work had to be sorted out by the estate staff, not least organising the use of the state coach. For most of the time we acted as a go-between and Edward would send people to the office with their instructions and we would direct them as necessary.

The foresters were engaged to tidy up the park and churchyard, Hawthorne was under orders to make the lawns look superb and the builders were employed to make the Folly ready for the Rumshotts' return from their honeymoon. There was a feeling of excitement on the estate, not just in anticipation of the wedding itself but perhaps because people felt it was the beginning of a new era. The viscount was settling down ready to take on, in due course, the responsibilities of his earldom.

We got to know Elizabeth during the period of their engagement as she was involved in the preparation of her new home at the Folly. It had been a typical bachelor's pad before, comfortable but needing those touches that somehow only a girl can add. She wanted many of the rooms redecorated, so extra furniture – raided from the attics at Rumshott – was required and gradually the house took on a new appearance. Although they would retain a London house it was good for morale on the estate that they were going to make the Folly their home.

The build-up to the wedding day was immense, not just because of the work at Rumshott but also because of the media interest. The presence of Their Royal Highnesses the Prince and Princess of Arnhustein was bound to create international news and for Elizabeth, who was from a typical middle-class family, the pressure was formidable. On the evening before their wedding I had just gone out of the back door of Rumshott House when I found her alone in the yard.

'Oh, hi, Elizabeth,' I said, surprised that she was not still at dinner with the congregated families in the dining room. 'What are you doing out here?'

'Hello, James,' she replied. She seemed withdrawn and on the verge of tears. 'I'm just trying to take it all in. I'm so nervous about tomorrow.' She pushed her long hair back from her face and put her hand on my arm. 'Do you think I'm going to be all right?'

I supposed being surrounded by princesses, earls, countesses and viscounts she needed that touch of reality from someone not closely involved with it all. From tomorrow she herself would become a viscountess, Lady Elizabeth.

'Of course you will,' I assured her, 'you'll be looking gorgeous and everyone will be wanting you to be happy. Don't worry. Just try to be yourself.'

'Thank you for that, James,' she said and turned back to rejoin her family. She was such a lovely girl I really hoped she would be happy. It must have been formidable just thinking about the forthcoming wedding,

The estate around Rumshott and Great Bassett was a hive of activity and the presence of the royals brought massive security measures. Policemen covering the area made it impossible to go anywhere near the park unless you had an identity pass and in addition to the uniformed constables at the gatehouses and patrolling the park walls, then-undercover colleagues were keeping the area under constant surveillance.

Officers armed with telescopic rifles would be stationed along the route that the royal party would travel, watching for the slightest threat to the meticulously planned day. Already the sniffer dogs had checked the house, the park, the drains, the cattle grids and the church. I always felt that there was something rather sinister and creepy about this aspect of being royal – it was the other side to the wealth, privilege and ceremonial splendour that most people saw.

On Saturday the paths to the church were packed with hundreds of people hoping to see the famous personalities arriving and of course, the stunning bride and her wedding dress, the design of which had remained a well-kept secret. The television and newspaper cameramen were fighting to get the best views and I felt very self-conscious walking up to the church door.

'Who's that?' I heard people ask as I went past. I hoped that I had been right telling Elizabeth she'd be okay – I felt nervous enough and I was only an unknown guest.

The church was packed with smartly dressed people filling the nave with life and happiness. An overwhelming abundance of beautiful flower arrangements brought colour and scent to one of the most elite congregations in the world that day. I recognised many famous people sitting there together with some of the estate staff and tenants when, with a triumphant salute the bride entered the church and the congregation rose to meet her.

She was wearing an exquisite dark ivory dress and her long train trailed behind, surrounded by

185

her bridesmaids. Despite her fears she looked radiant as she walked down the aisle with her father towards her future husband and the priest who was to marry them, His Grace the Archbishop of Canterbury.

After a moving and euphoric service accompanied by fanfares of trumpets, the state coach took the bride and groom back to Rumshott. I was silently praying that Lord Leghorn had not arranged for another highwayman to intercept them on the way as I could imagine that with all the police snipers about the unfortunate bandit could have been shot by mistake. But happily the earl had decided not to have a re-run and the newly married Viscount and Viscountess Rumshott proceeded to the house without harassment.

The reception was magnificent. The guests flowed through all the formal state reception rooms, waited upon by an army of servants bearing champagne and delicious food. It was Leghorn hospitality at its very best, which was frankly as good as you could hope to get. There was an awe-inspiring collection of guests – a vast assembly of some of the richest and most powerful people from all over the world. There were also plenty who were not rich, powerful or famous, like myself, so I was rather surprised when Lady Leghorn sat me next to the Archbishop of Canterbury. Perhaps she thought that I needed a little spiritual guidance but in fact as we sat there in one of the most opulent reception rooms in Europe, surrounded by the rich and famous, His Grace and I got involved in a long discussion about pig breeding. It was possibly one of the most extraordinary discussions I have ever had, particularly as I associated pigs with the likes of Gerald Birtwhistle and his ex-post office van.

Following the wedding, life on the estate quickly returned to normal. Everything seemed rather dead after the build-up to the great day and the huge number of people that had been around.

Suddenly we were out of the limelight, once more an ordinary country estate in the shires of England.

The following Monday, Lord Leghorn came in to see me. He was delighted at the way the wedding had gone.

'I w-wanted t-to send the Archbishop something,' he said, 'to t-thank him for coming to Rumshott.'

'Oh, that's a good idea, my lord. Have you thought what you might give him?'

'I thought we might send him a t-tree for him to plant in his garden, or maybe some rose bushes,' he suggested.

'Perhaps some rose bushes might be more suitable, my lord – after all we don't know how big his garden is.'

His lordship had a penchant for ordering specimen trees which was fine if you had a ten-acre arboretum attached to your garden but I suspected that the Archbishop's own home, rather than his official residence at Lambeth Palace, might not be as substantial as his lordship envisaged.

'Yes, yes, we'll get some roses. I'll order them

now. Could you telephone his wife and ask her where they would like them delivered p-please, and let me know.'

It isn't a straightforward affair trying to get hold of the Archbishop of Canterbury's wife and trying to explain to a considerable number of secretaries, or whoever they were at Lambeth Palace, about the proposed rose bushes didn't immediately open any doors. Eventually, however, I managed to speak to her and deal with his lordship's query.

Every now and then the earl would decide that he wanted to plant some particular species of tree and ask me to track down a supplier who could get hold of them for us. Sometimes they were planted in commemoration of an event such as Lord Rumshott's wedding, but more often than not they appeared for no reason at all. Hawthorne found the whole thing most irritating because not only did he have to look after them until they were established, but the little plaques that his lordship insisted on placing in the grass beside each tree made mowing awkward.

I would receive one of his lordship's memos on his Bond Street writing paper indicating the size of the plaque and lettering to be ordered. They were substantial bronze signs with heavy brass stakes and the Latin name for the tree would be embossed on it together with the date it was planted. They certainly looked smart when one walked around the arboretum at the side of the house, but I sympathised with Hawthorne who had to move them every time the grass was mowed. Even so I knew that one or two of them had ended up entangled in the lawnmower.

The arboretum was an area of the gardens where very few people walked and it was a beautiful and restful place in which to spend a few quiet moments. Gravel paths circled the lake with its secret island and the wonderful variety of trees displayed an astonishing array of colours throughout the year. Its most important draw for me was that the first daffodils would bloom there in the early spring, heralding the promise that a new summer was not far away and invigorating my hopes for the future.

## Chapter 21

I had been introduced to the Princess of Arnhustein at the Rumshotts' wedding and I sincerely hoped that she had not remembered me from the time we had met before, when I must have smelt like a well-used cat litter tray.

I had arranged to meet the nightwatchman to monitor how effective the security rounds were when the house was filled with guests. The princess was there on a private visit to her father but I had forgotten that as I spent the afternoon helping Tom Dagg dip his sheep. We had just finished the last batch of lambs when I remembered my appointment with the security man at the house.

'Oh, hell, Tom,' I exclaimed as I looked at my watch and saw it was ten to eight. 'I've got be at the house by eight.' I jumped into my car and shouted, 'I'll see you at the pub later for some supper,' as I sped off to Rumshott.

I didn't have time to notice that I was plastered in sheep muck – my clothes were covered in the stuff, it was stuck in my hair, ingrained under my fingernails and smeared over my face. I also smelt strongly of the noxious chemical which supposedly kill the sheeps' parasites and certainly made my eyes water as I drove to the house. It was one of those inevitable mistimings I suppose, but as I barged through the back door into the kitchen passage I nearly knocked Her Royal Highness flying. She stared at me in horror whilst I apologised profusely and made a sort of little bow. She was of course 'off duty' but her legendary warmth and friendliness soon surfaced, taking me by surprise.

Lady Leghorn could sometimes display similar kind feelings despite her famous temper and it was just as I was trying to work out how on earth I could afford about an acre of carpet for Harbottle Grange when I was summoned to her bedroom one morning.

'James,' she said, 'I gather you need some carpets.'

I was rather surprised that she knew anything about it as she didn't usually concern herself with such matters. 'Yes, my lady. I'm trying to sort out...'

'Well I don't know anything about it,' she interrupted, 'but there's a lot of carpet we took out of the private wing a few years ago which is up in the attic I believe. Now look, if you or Jocelyn can find it then by all means take what you want.'

I was practically speechless. Her ladyship took so little interest in estate matters I was surprised she had even registered the fact that I need any carpets.

'Well, um, Lady Leghorn. That's incredibly kind of you. I can't tell you how much I appreciate it. Thank you so much.'

'Find Jocelyn and go and have a search now,' she told me 'so you can start to sort things out. I can't imagine living in a house without carpets. Quite revolting and so uncivilised.'

Jocelyn had been forewarned and already located an attic room full of carpets stacked up in piles until they filled the room. There must have been enough there to carpet Harbottle two or three times over. Perhaps her ladyship did have a compassionate streak in her after all.

I was also trying to find some more furniture. I had been fortunate enough to inherit a number of antiques from my grandparents but the house needed a great deal more. As I could not afford to walk into a shop and buy what I needed I had taken to attending a monthly auction sale held in Russet where I would leave commission bids on particular pieces that I liked. It became a bit of a hobby of mine and I would spend the evening before the sale wandering around the auction room, catalogue in hand, deciding what to bid for. I would make a circuit marking down items of interest and then continue on a second circuit noting a price that I was prepared to pay. Finally I carefully examined the chosen pieces of furniture or paintings and adjusted my bid

191

accordingly. I had a pretty good idea of the value of most antiques but it was annoying that the auctioneers never put a guide price in the catalogues.

I only ever made one serious error of judgement in my valuations but it was particularly embarrassing because I had taken Sophie with me to the viewing evening. Amongst one or two other things I marked down in my catalogue was a set of five tatty but reasonably elegant chairs which I thought would be useful in the kitchen once the seats had been re-upholstered. On my second walk round I put a price of thirty pounds against them but on my final consideration I decided that perhaps twenty-five pounds for the set was enough and left the bid with the auctioneer.

Sophie thought that I was being a bit mean.

'Surely they're worth more than five quid a chair,' she suggested. 'I don't think you'll get them for that.'

'Well maybe not,' I agreed, 'but they need a lot spending on them don't they?'

She was not convinced.

The following afternoon I was working out the estate cottage valuation for insurance purposes with George. He had given strict instructions that we were not to be disturbed so before going up to his office I asked Sophie to give the auctioneers a ring at about four o'clock to find out about the pieces I had hoped to buy.

Just after four o'clock there was a rattling of china cups and a knock on the door.

'Come in,' shouted George fortissimo, making

me jump. He was in good spirits as we were making excellent progress on the valuation. 'Ah, Sophie, some tea. Marvellous.' She was carrying a tray with George's customary pot of Earl Grey, two cups and saucers and a little jug of milk. George was not a tea-bag-in-the-mug type and he always made a little ritual of pouring out the insipid brew even if I was the only onlooker.

Sophie had a smirk on her face and I guessed that it was to do with some excellent news from the auction.

'Did you phone the auctioneers?' I asked her hopefully.

'Er, yes,' she replied trying not to smile.

'Well what did I get?' I waited anxiously.

'Nothing I'm afraid.'

'Nothing? What, not even those old chairs?' It was not often that I did not pick something up.

'Ah,' she said gravely, 'especially not the chairs.'

'What did they make then?'

'You really embarrassed me there. They laughed at me down the phone.' She looked at George and explained. 'He left a bid of twenty-five pounds on a set of chairs that sold for £9,600.'

I was flabbergasted. '£9,600 for those chairs. Well I'll be damned.'

Of course they thought that this was hilarious and it was surprising how quickly the rest of the estate staff got to know about it. Even his lordship came in and remarked, 'I g-gather you w-were hoping to p-pick up a bargain at t-the sales!'

# Chapter 22

I'd had enough of rabbits and was not particularly pleased when PC Cripps arrived in the office first thing one morning to tell me that Betty Williams' bunny had been reported stolen.

Most days he would call in at the estate office for a cup of coffee, tell us the latest gossip, have a laugh with the girls and go off again on his patrols. He was not inclined to bother us with petty incidents on the estate so it was strange that he had come in about the rabbit.

'Morning, James,' he said.

'Ah, morning, Stan. How are you today?' I asked. I liked him calling in as it enabled us to maintain a good relationship with the police, sustained in the main by a copious supply of coffee and digestive biscuits.

'I'm fine, thanks. Just been up to sort out this drama at the post office,' he told me.

'What drama? Has there been a raid?' I imagined poor Mrs Ingels, the new postmistress being held up at gunpoint as the safe was ransacked. A fine start to her new job.

'Oh no no, nothing like that,' he assured me with a twinkle in his eye. 'It's far more serious. Miss Williams' rabbit's been stolen.'

I did not want to know about the misfortunes of our former postmistress. I had enough on my plate without getting drawn into some rabbit-themed farce.

'Oh, I don't believe it,' I sighed. 'Stan, please don't get me involved with Betty's rabbit.'

As an elderly spinster with no close family the rabbit had been dear to her heart. She used to talk about it whenever I went into the post office so I knew how important it was to her. But she had just retired and moved to a cottage near Rugby so I could not understand what on earth we had to do with the rabbit now.

'She's moved away, Stan. Are you sure you've got this right?'

'Ah, well,' he said knowingly, 'that's the problem. She moved but the rabbit didn't. They wouldn't take it in the removal lorry so Mrs Ingels said she'd look after it until someone could take it over for her.'

'Well, I expect it's just escaped,' I suggested, trying to dismiss the problem.

'It's a bloody strong rabbit if that's the case. It'll be carrying its hutch!'

'Oh, I see.' I was defeated. He was determined that I would be involved. 'So Mrs Ingels reported it stolen and that's all we know? There's really nothing I can do to help I'm afraid.'

'There is actually. I wondered if you'd be kind enough to break the news to Miss Williams for me,' he asked.

'Right, well I'll do that but that's it. I'm sorry, Stan, but I've got a lot on today.' I retreated into my office and dialled Betty's new number, wondering how I was going to break the news to her.

'Good morning, Betty, it's James Aden here. How are you settling in?' I started.

195

'Oh, hello, Mr Aden. It's so kind of you to ring. Funnily enough I was just thinking of you all up at Rumshott and saying to Eric how much we're going to miss you.'

'Well we're going to miss you too, you know. After all you were postmistress here for over forty years.' A sudden vague recollection crossed my mind. 'Betty, who's Eric?'

'Tut tut, Mr Aden. You can't have forgotten already. You know who Eric is, he's my rabbit!'

I breathed a sigh of relief and replied honestly, 'Of course I haven't forgotten about Eric. Actually I've only been thinking about him this morning.'

'Yes,' she continued, 'Mr Dodds at number four brought him round early this morning on his way to work. I had to leave him at the post office for a few days but Mr Dodds is ever such a kind man you know.'

I chatted with her for a while and then called Sophie.

'Sophie, could you be an absolute dear,' I asked her tongue in cheek, 'and go straight up to the post office and tell Stan Cripps that Detective Inspector Aden wants to see him in the estate office immediately.' She looked at me strangely. 'Detective Inspector?' she queried.

'I'll explain later,' I replied.

He came back fifteen minutes later. 'What's this Detective Inspector business?' he asked, grinning broadly.

'I've found Eric,' I told him.

'Who the bloody hell is Eric?'

I recounted the telephone conversation to him

and as he left he called out, 'I owe you one now, don't I?'

I turned my attention back to my work. I was in the midst of preparing the estate budgets for the following year, a tiresome and complicated business. The budgets were separated into various parts: the general estate; the forestry department; the shoot; the house; the home farm and each trust. Generally I had a fairly good idea of what to do. I could estimate reasonably accurately the annual income for each enterprise and then allocate expenditure against it, leaving a profit or loss depending on the requirements for that enterprise.

The one that I struggled with the most was the general estate budget. It was more or less definite what income there would be during the year from farm and cottage rents but the expenditure side was markedly less predictable. The problem was that the Leghorns regarded this account as a bottomless source of money and if they couldn't find the money elsewhere they delved into this account. The result was that not a year went past without the budgeted expenditure being exceeded by an alarming amount. It was absolutely impossible for me to guess what extraordinary ideas they might come up with next.

It was because of this overexpenditure that, as with many other estates in this country, the owners and more particularly their agents were always looking for new ways of improving income. The days when a landowner merely sat back and waited for the rents to come pouring in had gone and unfortunately many estate owners had not adjusted their lifestyles accordingly.

I had done some work towards finding new sources of income – by letting shoot days, making the deer more profitable and holding events in the park such as the horse trials and gun dog competitions. The Leghorns had their shop and the house was open to the public but these schemes were all of only limited help.

Every so often his lordship would come up with an idea and invariably ask me to look into it for him. His ideas varied from the possible to the outrageous. The word diversification appealed to him but sometimes it seemed as though he thought it meant obtaining money from the wildest dreams possible.

One of the more realistic projects that we looked at was bottling mineral water obtained from the natural springs in the park. It appeared that there were sufficient quantities to at least consider a production line and the necessary buildings could have been made available to house the bottling machinery at Lordspring-wood. It seemed feasible and his lordship was already imagining it stocked in his shop before I had had a chance to even have the suitability of the water tested.

His lordship decided to get involved on the practical side as he was so highly enthused by the idea and unfortunately, took it upon himself to set about designing the labels for the bottles.

'I-I've g-got some splendid ideas,' he told me one day, 'and I want to t-try to g-get them to complement the Rumshott labels.'

'Leave it t-to me, leave it to me!'

198

He had also, it transpired, been purchasing some very upmarket toiletries packaged in an extravagant-looking bottle with a fancy seal signed by the proprietor of the company. Unhappily, when his lordship sent over the draft labels the front looked excellent with a picture of Rumshott House overwritten with the legend RUMSHOTT SPRING WATER, but the little round gold seal that was supposed to be stuck on the back read GENUINE. PASSED BY THE EARL LEGHORN. I did not for one moment imagine that people would think that we were selling bottled urine but nonetheless it did not seem a useful marketing ploy.

However, in the end this did not matter as the water was tested and found to contain too many impurities to comply with the current European legislation and the idea, much to everybody's disappointment, was abandoned.

It had been a change for me to deal with clean water for once. Since becoming a resident agent I had spent an inordinate part of each day dealing with drains and sewage. I had quickly come to realise that most rural cottages and farmhouses were not connected to the main drains but relied on septic tanks or cesspits instead. Unfortunately, the responsibility for repairing these obnoxious structures lay with the landlord and as a result I spent an alarming amount of time with my head stuck down manholes trying to understand why the things had become blocked.

Luckily, the actual dirty work was dealt with by Dick Edwards, our self-employed odd job man. He was unpopular with Lou and the other girls because he liked to come into the office and report in great detail the findings of his blockages. He had a particular thing about condoms and firmly believed that they were the cause of most of his problems. But bar sending a note around to all the tenants suggesting that they used some other type of contraception, I really didn't think there was much we could do. One could always tell when he had been in the office because, despite Lou's attempts with an air freshener, a distinctive smell lingered long after he had gone. If he was not on the drains then I would sometimes give him some basic building tasks on the estate but he was predictably unsure of his work. Things he put up fell down, roofs he patched would leak and he could put the fear of God into me by saying, 'I'll guarantee it you know,' because if he said that, the only thing that was guaranteed was that it would go wrong.

## Chapter 23

It was about time to make a visit to Norfolk again. There was various building work going on, including the renovation of a couple of cottages, Mr Avery wanted to discuss something about the woods – I hadn't understood a word he'd said on the telephone – and Miss Pink had rung about her goats.

I wasn't very keen on seeing Miss Pink and her goats as they had been nothing but a nuisance ever since she had got them. We had inherited her on the death of her father when she succeeded to his tenancy of a smallholding in the centre of Weston Ferretts. Reginald Pink had been a typical Norfolk smallholder, keeping a few pigs and growing vegetables which he sold to local shops. However, Miss Pink preferred to push ahead, at the forefront of modern agriculture, as she liked to put it, and had established a small but troublesome herd of milking goats. She was an ardent supporter of the health benefits of goats' milk and had managed to build up a local clientele of like-minded customers. At first the estate had looked benignly on her venture and paid for the conversion of the old pig buildings into a milking shed for her goats. But as time went on she became more and more demanding, mainly in her requests for extra land which just wasn't available. The other local farmers were reluctant to help her because she tended to overdo her sales pitch, thus alienating potential customers. She had claimed that the milk increased your fertility but as she was a spinster with no apparent results to prove this additional power, I wondered how she had arrived at that conclusion.

I picked up the telephone in my office and dialled Sophie's extension.

'Hi, it's James. I wondered if you were free to come to Weston Ferretts with me on Friday?'

'Um, that's okay, I suppose,' she said. 'What have you got to do there?'

'Oh, see Avery, look at the High Street cottages and meet Miss Pink again.'

There was a brief silence.

'Do you need me for any of that?'

'Well, um, I thought it would be something different. You've hardly been up there since you've been at Rumshott. Also, um, I was hoping that perhaps we could stay on the coast for the weekend.'

There was another silence.

'Well?' I asked her.

'Look, can I come down and see you?'

'Okay. What's the matter?'

'I'll come down.'

She knocked on the door a few moments later and came in. I looked at her standing there, tall, slim, her vibrant blue eyes full of concern.

'What's the matter, Sophie?' I asked.

'Well,' she hesitated, 'it's you really. Of course I'd like to go to Norfolk with you but I never know where I am with you. Why do you want to stay up there for the weekend for a start?'

'I thought you'd like it. It'd be fun, a change. You know, somewhere different,' I explained lamely.

'It makes everything worse. Can't you see that? Spending time with you like that and then nothing happens. And if it does then suddenly you back off. Remember the point-to-point weekend. I have never felt so rejected in my whole life as I did after that night. You just, I don't know, you make me feel so worthless, so humiliated.'

I was silent. Of course I had guessed how she might be feeling but in my own selfish way I had merely glossed over it. She had every reason to talk like this. After the horse trials party I had realised exactly what I wanted from her, how

202

despite all my reservations of the past I was prepared to chance anything to be with her. It had taken the shock of seeing another man with her for me to realise it and now it seemed as though she was the one to hesitate.

'Sophie, I didn't mean to humiliate you. Believe me that's the last thing I want. I am really sorry for what's happened. What about our day at Wimbledon? We had a good time together then, didn't we? Can't we give this one more chance? It'll be different I promise you.'

She stared at me intently.

'Please, Sophie,' I pleaded, 'I'm sorry you have had such mixed messages.'

'Wimbledon was different. His lordship gave us the tickets so we had to go – it wasn't quite the same as you asking me out.' There was another silence. 'You know I really can't make you out sometimes. Why don't you sort yourself out and decide what you want out of life?'

'Well I'm asking you out now. Okay, we're going up there for work but I want to spend the weekend with you.'

'All right, we'll give it one last try. But this is the last time James.'

A few days later we drove over to Norfolk. There was a slightly awkward tension, a sense of being on trial, and it came as a relief to arrive at Weston Ferretts where we were met by Mr Avery.

'Good morning, Mr Avery. How are you today?' I asked.

'Ssalrit thanyou, Miseraden,' he said.

'This is Sophie, my assistant.'

He peered at her as though she was an alien

being and I could sense that the thought of a girl doing an agent's job was incomprehensible to him.

'Ssmorn t'you, mam.' He gave a little bow.

'Shall we go straight up to Primrose Hill and have a look at the problem you've got there?' I suggested. Long conversations with Mr Avery were not fruitful.

'Iis a right bloomnucking mess I can 'ell 'e.'

We followed him up the narrow flint-walled lane to the top of the hill where he came to an abrupt halt, causing me to nearly run into the back of his truck. Placing a grease-smeared trilby on his head he whistled to a couple of terriers that had shot off into a thicket of brambles.

'Buggasgorn ter ssabits,' he explained, which I took to mean they'd gone after some rabbits though Sophie, judging by the look on her face, thought he was speaking some foreign language.

'What's the problem you wanted to show me, Mr Avery?'

He led us into the wood, the dappled sunlight filtering through the leaves shading us from what was becoming a scorching summer's day.

'See ere bin deers snapt orf t'young'uns,' he said, pointing out some small trees that he had planted earlier that spring.

'Deer damage,' I translated for Sophie. 'They come in and bite the leading shoots off the trees. Completely useless now, they'll never grow into a decent shape.'

'Wha's t'be dun bout'it, eh, Miseraden?'

'How much damage is there?' I asked and we walked on to have a closer look. 'Mmm – it's

204

pretty bad. I'm afraid we're going to need to fence this area to keep the deer out and then replant in the autumn. No other practical way around it.'

'Yea, thowt as much m'self. You wanme t'put up t'ence?'

'Yes please, if you can fit it in some time over the summer. Better send me a price beforehand.'

We left him pacing out the measurements and called in on the builders at the cottages. For once they were running to schedule and before long we were on our way to Miss Pink's.

We arrived in the middle of a drama – one of her billy goats had escaped and gone on the rampage in next door's garden. By some extraordinary feat of lateral thinking she put the blame on me.

'If the estate had let me some more land this would never have happened,' she exploded.

'There is no more land available Miss Pink. I've explained this a hundred times before. There just isn't anything I can do about it.'

'Are you anti-goats like Mr Aden?' she asked a startled Sophie.

'It's nothing to do with being anti-goats,' I interrupted. 'Surely you can understand the position.'

It was pretty hopeless really. I felt that I was banging my head against a brick wall and I resolved not to visit her again unless it was to review an increase in the rent.

The distractions of the day had relieved the tension between Sophie and myself and so with a mounting sense of excitement we set off for Brancaster. This would be the first time that we

205

had been together away from the estate and from work.

We booked into an old smugglers' inn, the Creek Hotel in Brancaster Staithe on the north Norfolk coast. The inn was a stone's throw from the river running out into the North Sea and the glorious summer weather had brought many weekenders and sailors to the busy little village.

Sophie and I were unconcerned with the crowds and as soon as we had been shown to our room nestling under the eaves of the thatch we embraced with fervour. No inhibitions, no sense of unease or guilt. Finally it seemed as though we were free to be together. There was no holding back and our union was at once tender, forceful and complete.

Later, as Sophie lay with her eyes closed, I watched her, wondering how I could ever have doubted the way forward. I held her in my arms, stroking her hair, her cheeks, gently kissing her forehead. The sensation of touching her face was one of unbelievable calm and love.

We spent the weekend in a trance wrapped up in our own company simply wanting to be together. We walked along the vast sandy beaches of Holkham, sailed a little boat along the river, ate superb fresh fish and drank some delicious wines.

At night we made love in a room laden with ancient oak beams which embraced us within a secret place – somewhere that had finally brought us together.

# Chapter 24

Returning from Norfolk in a state of heady emotion I was abruptly brought down to earth by a note on my desk the following morning. 'Please see Lord Leghorn immediately,' it read.

I went over to the house to find his lordship finishing a late breakfast and poking desultorily at the lone kipper on his plate. He looked up with relief when I entered the room.

'Oh, I'm sorry, my lord,' I said. 'I didn't realise you were still eating.'

'N-no, not at all. Come in. I w-wanted to s-speak to you, James.'

'Yes, I got your note, my lord. What's happened?'

'Nothing's h-happened as such,' he explained, 'but I was talking to a f-friend in Gloucestershire, and he was t-telling me that we should g-get a better c-computer. These n-newest ones save a lot of work, you know.'

'Oh,' I said, rather surprised. I didn't think his lordship knew much about computers and unashamedly I knew little more. We had one in the office but I had an inherent distrust of it and only used it for the most basic tasks. George had brought up the subject before and knowing my views had accused me of being happy with 'pulling a goose's feather from its arse and dipping it in ink', which was not only unfair but inaccurate.

'So I t-think you should go and b-buy one,' his lordship continued. 'You c-can probably get t-them in one of those electrical places in Russet.'

From the little I did know I suspected that it was a bit more involved than buying something like a toaster but it was no good discussing the finer points with his lordship.

Within a month a sophisticated new computer had arrived at the estate office. For a while it lurked menacingly on a large Jacobean table in the corner of Sophie's office and there it would have stayed if George hadn't intervened.

'Have you plugged the bloody thing in yet?' he asked one morning.

'Haven't had time, I'm afraid,' I replied.

'Well, there's no point in having the damned thing unless you do, is there?'

'No, no, there's not. Um – I suppose we'd better get someone over to show us what to do,' I suggested.

'What do you mean, show us what to do? Can't you put a plug on? Get the bloody thing out and I'll do it myself.'

'George, it's a bit more involved than that. It's not just putting a plug on. We've got to know how to use it – you know the software and hardware or whatever. It's much more complicated than the other one.'

He started rummaging around in the box and found the instruction booklet.

'Look, it'll all be in here,' he exclaimed in triumph. 'This'll tell you what to do.'

I looked at him in exasperation. 'George, please, leave me to arrange for someone to come and provide training. I'm quite happy to use the machine but we need an expert to set it up.'

In due course a very helpful and understanding lady arrived and managed to introduce me to the latest idiosyncrasies of computer technology. I still couldn't fathom why something made of hard plastic and as rigid as a Royal Doulton dinner plate should be called floppy but eventually I overcame my distrust and accepted the machine as no more than an accountant's lawnmower.

One of the most immediate effects it had on the estate was to render the fortnightly trips to the bank obsolete. Instead of collecting the wages in cash, the computer paid them directly into the staff's accounts. I missed that routine but the idea of collecting up to £15,000 in cash now seemed foolhardy. The same routine had been in existence for years and had been a vulnerable target for robbery. At five-past nine every other Thursday, Nugent, the semiretired clerk of works, would draw up outside the estate office in his old blue Land Rover and clamber up the steps clutching a worn leather briefcase, which gaped open along one end where the stitches had come undone. It was odd that Nugent should have been appointed to this particular job because he was one of the least agile men on the estate. Seventy years old, he suffered from terribly arthritic hips, poor hearing and bad eyesight. In the event of having to act quickly, he would most certainly have been at a disadvantage.

Wendy would hand him the breakdown sheet stating exactly what was to be collected, having telephoned the bank in advance so that it would all be ready on our arrival, and we would then set off for Russet in the Land Rover. As Nugent's eyesight prevented him travelling anywhere that he might encounter traffic lights, I drove.

The route we followed never varied. Our first stop was at the baker's in the High Street where I was despatched to purchase a selection of cakes for the Nugent household. Nugent meanwhile would sit in the Land Rover with the doors locked, despite the fact that the money we were carrying at that point was only enough to pay for the cakes, and stare menacingly out of the window at any passers-by. Even children in pushchairs did not escape his vivid scrutiny as he tried to memorise the features of potential thieves intent on stealing his leather case.

Once the cake box, secured with a length of royal-blue ribbon, had been safely wedged on to the middle seat of the Land Rover we continued to the bank, parking in exactly the same spot at exactly the same time as always. Both of us would then enter the bank, Nugent on the constant lookout for bandits, and collect the cash. Having stuffed the bags of money into the briefcase, Nugent would march out of the bank as quickly as he could, the weight of the bag accentuating his painful limp, with me just behind.

It must have been my youthful inexperience which led to his accusations of kidnap. Ever since my first trip to the bank with Nugent I had felt that it was my responsibility to reduce the risk of robbery and so on one occasion I took an alternative route home. It was a dreadful mistake. I have never seen a man so quickly overcome by terror. Despite the fact that I was munching happily on a warm sausage roll that I had bought at the bakery and the Land Rover was struggling to do more than twenty miles an hour up a hill, he took the view that I was making a getaway. The distress I caused him was enough to prevent me from doing it again, and on reflection I thought that he was far more likely to die from a heart attack than be killed in a hold up.

Although it was vital to keep up with advances in technology I relished the timelessness of the historic buildings and landscapes which formed my working environment. One moment I might be in the grandeur of the state rooms, the next be out at an appointment in the allotment gardens. The diversity of work on a rural estate meant that one never took the privilege for granted. At the beginning of my career I had assumed that my skills of tact and diplomacy would be most tested when dealing with the English aristocracy – I couldn't have been more mistaken. The allotment gardeners outranked them all.

Dating back to the early 1800s, the allotment gardens on the estate were large vegetable patches which formed part of the landholding of the lord of the manor of Rumshott. Generally they were rented by a gentle group of people quite content with pottering among their vegetables and end-lessly erecting sheets of corrugated iron into what might loosely be described as sheds. But there were hundreds of the things dotted over the estate and the amount of trouble they caused me was disproportionate to the land they occupied or the rental income they produced. Many a wasted hour was spent examining some compelling evidence of a few torn cabbage leaves as I hovered uncertainly between two gnarled-fingered allotment holders persuading them to lay down their spades and come to a more reasoned solution.

There was one other group of people who invoked similar feelings and they were the visitors to the house. Although Rumshott was open nearly every day of the year, the busiest time, of course, was the summer. The tourist season began at Easter when the first coachloads of visitors would arrive. My feelings were always mixed, the anticipation of spring tinged by the knowledge that with the tourists came trouble. The sight of fifty elderly ladies disembarking from a coach tended to drive me inside the office quicker than a downpour of rain. From the safety of my lair I would watch groups of weekday visitors ignoring signposts and wandering about like lost sheep. Bunches of women, shrouded in those peculiarly unfashionable nylon raincoats that resemble the wrappings from a new refrigerator, traipsed aimlessly around the stableyard clutching plastic carrier bags, which presumably contained their sandwiches and a Thermos of tea. The end result was always the same. Lady Leghorn would catapult out of her tearoom and shout at them as though they were deaf.

'No,' she would bellow, 'that is the house over there,' and gesticulate wildly in the direction of Rumshott House. How anyone could not notice a mansion a hundred yards in front of them was beyond my comprehension.

They did other annoying things like fall over or

leave belongings behind. Lord and Lady Leg-horn would spend ages chatting to then-visitors in the hope of eventually selling a packet of fudge or perhaps even a fake diamond tiara. Their positions in society must have prepared them to accept these duties as being all in the course of a day's work and I admired their patience.

There was one bright side to the visitors' presence and that was the abundant supply of delicious home-made cakes that we were able to pilfer from the tearoom. Sophie had taken on the unofficial responsibility of making friends with the teashop ladies so that she could purloin some delicacies for consumption in the estate office when she had the chance, a skill that took a while to perfect. Early in Sophie's cake career she had had the misfortune to return triumphantly to the office with a particularly gooey chocolate gateau – a certain winner amongst the rest of us – only to find her ladyship in the reception hall. In the ensuing fracas we were blamed for the unprofit-ability of just about everything including, some-what inaccurately, the current recession in the domestic tourism industry.

## Chapter 25

George could always be heard coming down from his office quite some while before he reached the reception hall. His descent was accompanied by a lot of crashing and the vibrations of the battered

213

stairs shuddering through the building. On this particular morning there was a moment's deathly silence when he reached the bottom which was shattered by the cry, 'What on earth is that bloody awful smell?'

Louise rushed out of her office with her hand over her mouth.

'I'm afraid the Pringles have just been in, Mr Pratt,' she explained.

'Oh, God,' he exclaimed, 'haven't those damned people learnt to wash yet? It's a bloody disgrace.'

Wendy, the accountant, who was particularly sensitive over matters of hygiene and cleanliness, came out of her office clutching an aerosol of air freshener.

'I keep this for when they come in,' she said, spraying vigorously around the hall and inadvertently blasting George with a good dose of pot-pourri.

'Mind out,' he said leaping sideways, 'I don't want to smell like a bunch of dead flowers all day.'

Then the front door opened and his lordship ambled in on the scene seemingly oblivious to the unusual sight of his agent being sprayed with air freshener.

'B-bloody awful p-pong in here, you know, George. Something died?'

'Ah, morning, my lord,' said George, spinning round. 'Just trying to get rid of it actually – Pringles have been in, I'm afraid.'

'Dear oh d-dear. They are the most re-revolting people. Can't understand why they don't wash themselves.'

214

'I quite agree, my lord. Smells like a cat's crapped in the cupboard. Dread to think what their cottage is like.'

Unfortunately I knew exactly what their cottage was like as I had visited often enough, in order to sort out a steady trickle of problems. In fact I had been there only a week before dealing with what in any circumstances would have been an unpleasant task and in their case was utterly vile. They had, so they informed me over the phone, a leaking lavatory pan.

With hundreds of let cottages to look after I came across an alarming number of problems to do with lavatories. I generally accepted it as part of the job and, having become acquainted with an infinite array of colours, styles, makes and ages, had come to consider myself something of a lavatory expert. Distressingly, I had also come across varying standards of cleanliness, from the spotless white porcelain to those that had all manner of bits and pieces floating in them, stuck to them and, most frighteningly of all, scattered around them. The Pringles' lavatory fell into the last category.

Before calling at the Pringles' cottage I had prayed fervently that it would be a quick, simple visit and that I would not need to draw breath once inside the house. I had become quite adept at this and regarded a visit in the same way I regarded a deep dive under water, the need to hold my breath paramount. I suppose they must have found me a bit odd as I would enter their house, rush around at speed not uttering a sound and then leave with a red face and bulging eyes, gasping for air once I'd returned outside.

I entered the bathroom despondent and left nauseated. Without thinking I had drawn breath, mesmerised by the carnage in front of me. It was like witnessing a particularly bad car accident. The Pringles' bathroom was the most distressing, odour-filled nightmare of a bathroom fatality that I had ever seen.

Reeling from the shock I tumbled headway down the narrow stairs, grabbing the grease-covered handrail as a support. I struggled valiantly to the front door whereupon I collapsed gasping for fresh air and hoping that my nerves had not been permanently damaged.

To the Pringles it must have seemed like an ordinary visit from the deputy agent who appeared to be suffering from a chronic asthma attack. They all clustered around me waiting for the verdict on the leaking lavatory pan. I had decided that the only remedy was to demolish the house, probably with the Pringles inside and it was some while before I could begin to contemplate a less drastic solution. They continued to hover over me patiently and indeed they were not an unkindly lot. They were staunch supporters of a Baptist church in Russet and always attended local fundraising events in the village, although I gathered Mrs Pringle's home-baked cakes were never great sellers on the produce stall.

Once the blood supply had resumed its normal course to my brain I became aware of a rather delicate problem to do with the bathroom and one that I did not know how to solve. My studies

216

at the Royal Agricultural College had taught me about leaking lavatories but not one of our lecturers had ever explained how to toilet train an entire family.

In a desperate act of cowardice I am ashamed to admit that I crept away down the garden path offering the only possible solution.

'I'll get the plumber to call round and fix it,' I muttered, waving apologetically to the assembled family.

It was with the pungent aroma of the Pringles lingering in the estate office that Lord Leghorn requested that I visit her ladyship in the house that afternoon. Coincidentally she was having some problems with sanitation on one of her projects. Needless to say her concerns were on a different scale to those of the Pringles.

After lunch I walked across the manicured lawns towards the house and, being a little early for my appointment, detoured through the gardens in order to enjoy the spring fragrances of the early flowers which were blossoming in the warm sunshine. In spite of Hawthorne's reluctance to dismount from the seat of his lawnmower he maintained enough flower borders to provide a splash of colour throughout the year. I crunched along the trimmed gravel paths until I found a French window open on the north front.

The north side of Rumshott contained some of its finest state rooms. I entered the Gainsborough Room whose intricately ornate gilded ceiling, massive carved marble fireplace and polished oak floor housed one of the finest private collections of Gainsborough's paintings anywhere in the

217

world. It was a privilege to be able to wander through these rooms.

Reluctantly I turned away from the paintings and went in search of her ladyship. I was supposed to be meeting her in the Oak Dining Room but her instructions turned out to be somewhat vague. I finally found her in his lordship's study, bombarding her husband with a barrage of problems to do with what she called the Bailiffs' Room Flat.

The flat was a series of rooms which lay as an out wing on the east end of the house and had once housed the archives of the family and estate. The archives were a veritable mine of information for students of Leghorn family history and it had caused an upset when some years previously her ladyship had sold them off. A unique treasure had been lost to the family for ever but more to the point, having apparently forgotten these rooms existed Lady Leghorn had recently rediscovered them, unused and abandoned, giving her the inspiration for a new project.

Her projects involved months of disruption, caused terrible rows, upset his lordship and cost a phenomenal amount of money although, to be fair, her ladyship had a superb flair and the end result would invariably be a triumph of design, style and luxury. No expense would be spared on the building alterations required, the furnishings, fabrics or paintings and the most fashionable London designers and decorators would be employed to achieve her ambitious plans.

We always ended up getting involved, firstly because there would be a summons issued by her

218

ladyship requiring the estate workmen to help. This signified the beginning of the rows. They did not sit in the workshop all day drinking tea waiting for something to do as she insisted on thinking. They had extremely busy and demanding schedules to follow in order to maintain the hundreds of other houses and buildings spread around the estate. The workload was immense for the number of men employed so when a project was thrust upon us everything else would fall apart. The frail elderly widows' cries of despair as they hoped for a single radiator to be installed were no match for the wrath of Lady Leghorn once a project was underway.

The second reason we got roped in was money, or the lack of it. The carefully budgeted accounts would be shattered as she did not adhere to any form of financial constraints. The Bailiffs' Room Flat had already cost £50,000 and wasn't halfway completed so there was a certain amount of nervousness on my part at being asked to sort out whatever sanitary problems her ladyship was experiencing.

'Ah, darling,' she beamed at me as I entered he study. 'I'm so glad you're here. Lordship's very concerned that we get the right baths for the flat, you know.'

His lordship wouldn't have been the least concerned about the baths, it was a ploy often used by her ladyship to encourage our hesitant support in her schemes.

She continued, 'Now you remember the ones we have in our bathrooms? We want those, two more exactly the same. I think they came from

Greece or somewhere Mediterranean didn't they darling?' she continued, her bouffant hair casting a shadow on the thick Wilton carpet.

I remembered the drama we'd had with those baths. 'I believe they are Italian, Lady Leghorn, and I seem to recall we had quite a job getting hold of them at the time.'

'Well, can you get some more and we simply must have them, MUST you hear me, by the end of next week.'

I hadn't realised the project was so urgent.

'Well I'll do what I can, Lady Leghorn, and let you know the position.'

I sprinted up the staircase to the private wing of the house where the Leghorns had their bedroom suites. I wanted to remind myself what the baths looked like and hopefully find the makers' name displayed.

The Leghorn's private bathrooms reflected their characters and predictably, when we had renovated them the previous year it had been her ladyship's that had been the most problematic. It wasn't as though his lordship's was plain – it was just that the grandeur was understated. The huge bath in the centre of the room was the size of a small swimming pool but it had chrome taps, admittedly as large as the ones normally seen on the back of a fire engine, but they were chrome. Her ladyship had insisted on gold-plated ones. His room smelt of the fresh air that breezed through the open window and gentlemen's aftershave, hers was hot enough to hatch a brood of pheasant chicks and engulfed me with an almost tangible soup-like concoction of aromatic disasters.

I discovered that although made by the same maker the two baths were not identical. One was plain while the other had fancy handles and ornate indentations for holding soap. I returned to the study with my observations.

I knocked on the heavy panelled door and was greeted with her ladyship shrieking, 'Go away, go away whoever you are. I'm in a meeting with his lordship it's very important and I AM NOT TO BE DISTURBED.'

Fortunately, I bumped into her ladyship's secretary as I crept along the passage towards the kitchens.

'Ah, Fenella,' I said in relief, 'you have heard about these damned baths no doubt? Well the two upstairs are different so I can't order them until I know which one her ladyship wants. Could you sort it out because she won't open the door at the moment.'

'Oh, dear, I'll see what I can do?' Fenella promised.

Once back in the office I dug out the invoice for the baths we'd bought the previous year and got hold of the supplier. A month's notice was required pre-delivery no matter what style of bath was being requested. Even for Lady Leghorn. I steeled myself for the forthcoming explosion and telephoned Fenella.

Ten minutes later her ladyship was on the phone.

'I want those baths this week,' she screamed. 'I will NOT WAIT a bloody month for them. Do they know WHO they're for?'

'Yes, I have told them Lady Leghorn but...'

'I'll get the damn things myself then. What's their number?'

I gave her the number.

'Did you speak to the managing director or some little man they employ?'

'I just spoke to their ordering department, it's not that they weren't helpful but they order them from Italy, which you may remember from...'

'I don't care if they come from Timbuktu. IF I WANT BATHS THEN I EXPECT THEM WHEN I SAY.'

I did not refer to the incident again although I heard from the housekeeper that the baths did arrive within her ladyship's demands but the wrong ones were delivered. By the time the correct baths arrived six weeks had passed.


# Chapter 26

I had been thrown into a frenzy of organisation by the arrival of a large white envelope on my doormat at Harbottle Grange Farm. After an early start feeding the animals I was sitting down to a hearty breakfast of bacon and eggs when the postman sauntered past the kitchen window.

'Morning, Bernard,' I called, 'anything interesting today?'

'Looks like you've got a stiffy in here,' he replied. Bernard maintained a healthy interest in the letters he delivered and over the years had developed an uncanny ability to determine their contents. Postcards were undeniably his favourites and he was able to tell us that it had been raining in Tenerife or was ninety degrees in the shade on Corfu without leaving Russetshire.

A stiffy, I had learnt, was a posh invitation and I slit open the envelope with anticipation to find 'James Aden and partner are invited by the Masters of the Woodland Farmers' Hunt to a Ball on Friday 16th November.'

I had already been to a couple of these wonderful annual parties held in a massive marquee on the lawns of a grand country house a few miles from Rumshott. Attended by an interesting mix of people, the guests all adhered to traditional custom and dressed in formal evening wear, bestowing on the event the elegance of a bygone era. The Leghorns were not hunting people even though previous earls had been masters of the hunt and so did not attend the ball, but many of their farming tenants would be out in force, representing the close relationship between the hunt and the estate.

Custom decreed that private dinner parties were to be hosted at home before going on to the ball for dancing at eleven o'clock. Thank goodness I was now going out with Sophie as I had invited a group of twelve friends and I needed all the help I could get with the entertaining.

Harbottle Grange was built for parties. The stone-flagged halls echoed with the sounds of laughter and music, the great table in the green dining room was laid with silver and crystal which reflected the leaping flames of the fire crackling in the grate.

The table itself was heavily connected with

Rumshott. During my visits to the auctions trying to find furniture I had been looking for a dining table large enough to do justice to the grand dining room. I soon realised that a decent table would cost more than I could afford and but for a chance find in the estate yard, I would still have been eating off an eight by four sheet of chipboard delicately balanced on a couple of old trestles.

The day of my trip to the estate yard started badly, with a surprisingly early call from her ladyship shortly after I'd arrived in the office.

'Where is Archie?' she asked.

'I'm not sure, Lady Leghorn,' I replied, 'is there something wrong?'

'Yes. There is the most terrible draught coming in under my bedroom door and unless you want me to die of cold I need him to fix it straightaway.'

I agreed to find him but when I received no answer from the telephone at his workshop I thought that I could leave the matter until after lunch. I imagined that the same draught had been coming under the door for the past five hundred years and a couple of extra hours were neither here nor there. An hour later I was proved wrong.

'It's her ladyship on the phone for you, James,' said Louise.

'Oh, hell, does she know I'm in?'

'I'm afraid so.'

'Okay, I'll take it.'

'WHERE is Archie?' she demanded. 'I rang you AN HOUR AGO and he's still not here.'

'I'm sorry, Lady Leghorn, but I haven't found him yet. He doesn't seem to be in his...'

'You must know where he is. It's your job to know where he is. You look after the men. FIND HIM. I am ABSOLUTELY FREEZING in here. I can't get out of bed it's SO BLOODY COLD. This is intolerable. No one should be expected to live in such conditions.'

I envisaged her lying in her heavily ornate seventeenth-century four-poster bed, surrounded by the dazzling collection of priceless master-pieces which adorned the silk damask-covered walls of her bedroom. Over in the far corner, about half a tennis court's length away next to the carved marble fireplace, her secretary would be sitting at a small William and Mary rosewood writing desk checking her ladyship's diary for the day.

'It must be awful Lady Leghorn. Quite dread-ful. I'll drive over to the yard and get Archie straight away.'

It was far less trouble to succumb to her de-mands and drive over to Maplethorpe where the joinery workshop was situated than face another conversation with her.

I did not particularly want to leave the comfort of the office. It was a typically miserable English winter day with heavy grey skies, constant penetrating rain and a cold blustery wind.

'Lou, I'm going out to find Archie,' I shouted as a gust of wind wrenched the door from my hand.

I ran across the stableyard to my car which had been coated in a thin layer of sodden beech leaves and larch needles. Irritatingly, some became wedged under the windscreen wipers and blurred my vision so, braving the elements again, I climbed out to clear them. Even the honey-coloured walls of the village cottages mirrored the bleakness of the weather, the rain turning the stone dark and grey like the sky. I hoped that I would find Archie in his workshop and not have to continue driving around in such morbid conditions. The fact that he hadn't answered the telephone didn't necessarily mean that he wasn't there. He said he often couldn't hear the phone because of the noise from a saw or lathe but I suspected he didn't hear it because he didn't want to – he wasn't keen on ladyship's summonses from the house.

Sure enough he was ensconced in his little office with a sales representative from one of the timber companies that supplied the estate with building materials. While they finished their discussion I went for a poke around the yard. Separate from the main builder's yard in the park, it was left relatively undisturbed and was now full of rubbish. Archie would never throw anything away and having worked there for forty years the accumulation was impressive. If one looked hard enough though, it was possible to discover the odd item of interest. I came across an old church pulpit, a sailing dinghy and even a horse-drawn hay cart. But the greatest discovery solved my table problem. I found a dead oak tree. It wasn't simply a dead oak tree, it had been carefully sawn into long planks and stacked, each piece separated from the next by little wedges, allowing it to season and dry out. With an idea forming rapidly in my mind I rushed off to find Archie and curtail his waffling with the rep.

'Archie, have you finished? I want you to have a look at something with me.'

Archie had a habit of dragging out a conversation to unbelievable lengths and I noticed his visitor make a hurried and I thought joyous sprint for his car.

'What is this oak butt for?' I asked, hoping it wasn't destined for some future project.

'Oh, that's been there for years,' he said and began a long discourse on its life history.

'That was a beautiful oak that grew in the park,' he explained, 'probably about four hundred years old when it blew down in a gale some fifteen years ago. I remember it was a Tuesday and the old earl...'

He knew exactly where it had stood on a rise above Rumshott House, how they had brought it back to Maplethorpe, who had helped him saw it into planks, in fact the only thing he didn't know was the man who had planted it.

It was a terrific find. A four-hundred-year-old oak, grown in Rumshott Park and air dried for fifteen years – perfect for highclass furniture making.

'Archie, do you think you could make me a dining table from it if I gave you a design?' I was enamoured by the idea and I hoped my enthusiasm was infectious.

'Don't see why not,' he said thoughtfully. 'In fact I'd quite like the chance to make a bit of furniture again. Make a change from repairing things.'

That reminded me of the original purpose of my visit and so I sent him off to see Lady Leghorn's draught but not before confirming the plan.

I duly purchased the timber from the estate, drew up a design with Archie based on a traditional late mediaeval refectory table and over the following months he worked at it during the evenings and weekends. He turned the legs on his lathe, sawed and planed, cut and dowelled until at last he had created a superb, beautiful piece of furniture. It became one of my most prized possessions and the only one that had its roots in the actual soil of Rumshott.

We sat around this great table the evening of the hunt ball, Sophie at one end and myself at the other, separated by several yards of oak planking and my guests. It made a huge and welcome difference having Sophie's help and although I had become quite adept at managing dinner parties in my bachelor existence, a girl's hand seemed to add a certain touch that somehow I could not achieve. Since leaving college I had progressed from meals that relied heavily on the contents of a tin to delicious casseroles of pheasant breasts soaked in brandy and cream, fresh vegetables and sautéed potatoes. Pheasant was a staple food during the winter but meals were occasionally enlivened by the appearance of a partridge or duck – depending on the contents of the weekly bag from the shoot.

I did not fare so well at puddings, allowing Sophie a free reign in concocting a creation involving raspberries, cream, meringues and honey.

She said that she'd made it before but after the third telephone call to her mother in Yorkshire and overhearing something about egg whites I did wonder.

The house felt like a proper home. All the beds were made up for the dozen guests, fires were burning in the reception rooms, there was plenty of noise and delicious aromas wafted from the Aga. It seemed a pity to leave it behind when the taxis arrived to take us over to the ball at Grittlesham Hall.

The scene on our arrival soon changed that. The marquee was filled with activity and a band was playing by the dance floor at the far end near our allocated table which was already set for breakfast. Several bottles stood open as we took our places to watch the first brave people take to the dance floor and started on the wine. The night flew past, dance after dance followed by a rest and a drink, more dancing, chatting with friends and finally breakfast to boost flagging energy. I danced with Sophie most of the time and during the last few slow dances of the evening it felt wonderful holding her so closely, knowing her so well and having someone to love. She looked stunning in her ball gown, her long dark hair tied up, her eyes sparkling. Her tall slim body pressed against mine as we circled the dance floor and with our inhibitions dimmed by the influence of alcohol we held each other tightly and kissed passionately, ecstatically happy in each others' company.

My great fear that a relationship with her would affect my work at the estate office had turned out to be unfounded – the only change it made was that I had to alter the selection process for cottage tenants. Up until then the system had been quite straightforward – interview three or four hopefuls from the waiting list, obtain references and then let to the prettiest girl. Sophie had noticed the increased number of attractive young ladies in the villages and commented that as we were going out together it might be tactful to expand the criteria for suitable tenants.

## Chapter 27

Sophie and I had decided to keep our relationship quiet, though not secret, on the estate and as people were used to seeing us together anyway, it did not pose a particular problem. The one person who had noticed our closer attachment was Charlie Blake, a tenant farmer on the northern edge of the estate who kept a herd of dairy cows.

At the time I was planning to build a new milking shed for him and so I was making frequent visits to his farm in order to design the modern replacement. Sophie had helped measure up the site on our previous meetings and he seemed surprised when he realised that she was more than just the office assistant. It certainly surprised his mother who was always questioning me on my romantic status, concerned apparently that I had no one to look after me. She was rather old-fashioned and believed that no man could exist without the help of a good woman. When she heard the news from Charlie she rather embarrassingly served up what she called a celebratory tea on our next visit.

The Blakes had a terribly poor farm on the stoniest, least productive land on the estate. It was doubly unfortunate as it stood at the top of an exposed piece of Russetshire countryside where the wind never stopped blowing. It must have been a healthy place to live though as they had farmed there for fifty years and Mrs Blake was still fit and well in her eighties. She liked to recount how her husband had died on the job aged ninety-two. My initial admiration and surprise at this feat was somewhat diluted when I found out she meant in the milking parlour amongst his cows.

The concern that Mrs Blake showed to me must have been due in part to her failure to get Charlie married off. He was still single at sixty and I imagine she'd rather given up hope. So the celebratory tea held an important part in her social calendar. It took place on one of those stunning early winter breaks in the gloom when the sun shines in a cloudless blue sky and the wind, although cold and unremitting, is fresh and invigorating. Normally if I called in at High Hill Farm for a cup of tea, I would be seated on an old sagging armchair by the Rayburn usually occupied by a large tabby cat whose hairs would remain stuck to my trousers for days afterwards. This time we were ushered into the front room where Charlie had laid a fire and Mrs Blake had set an enormous high tea. There were sandwiches with the crusts cut off, scones and jam, biscuits and a home-made fruitcake with a top the colour of polished mahogany. For an instant I feared that she had misunderstood the situation and thought Sophie and I were getting married but I was reassured when she explained that in part it was a thank you for helping Charlie with his new building.

This building had long been due an overhaul as he was still using a contraption called a milking bail which was no more than a corrugated iron hut on wheels under which the cows stood, six at a time, to be milked. Bails had been designed in the days of hand milking and although Charlie had rigged up a basic arrangement using a milking machine the whole thing was extremely rickety and inefficient. His red, gnarled hands bore witness to the basic nature of his machinery and it was only a matter of time before health and safety regulations would have closed the operation down. The delay in modernising High Hill Farm was entirely due to their reluctance to throw anything away or change it from the days of old Mr Blake. Never had I seen so much clutter assembled in one place. Mr Blake's car, an old rusty blue Ford Prefect, hadn't been moved from the drive where he had left it the day he died four years earlier. The old man's passion for saving all manner of bits and pieces had been ingrained into his family and neither Charlie nor his mother had been overenthusiastic when I first suggested building a new parlour. It had only been upon the insistence of the Milk Marketing Board that progress was at last being made. I had hoped that I might also persuade them to tidy up some of the scrap machinery lying around the yard but Charlie patiently explained the potential future use of each item. I failed to see how a horsedrawn turnip hoe could ever come in useful, as they neither had a horse nor grew turnips.

But stay it all did and I came to hold the Blakes in some affection. They were an unusual pair and whilst most of my farm visits meant discussing cashflow and computerised accounts with the farmers, at High Hill we talked about Bluebell's calf or Daisy's pendulous udder.

Having been detained so long we only just made it back to the office before closing time. George was pacing about in the hall.

'Where the bloody hell have you been?' he cried, having worked himself up into a frenzy. His face was red as he groped for his inhaler, an asthma attack looming. These always came on when he was under stress, although rather obscurely he blamed them on an allergy to mushrooms.

'Over at High Hill,' I explained, 'sorting out the Blakes' new parlour.'

'Well, bugger their parlour,' he exploded. 'What about my car?'

'Oh, George, sorry, I'd completely forgotten.' I was supposed to take him to fetch it from the garage in Russet where it was being serviced.

'Is it too late to go now?'

'Yes. You'll have to lend me yours and get Sophie to drop you home.'

'Okay, sorry about that,' I said, handing him the keys as he shot out the door. 'George, there's not much petrol in it,' I called after him but he had already disappeared.

'Well, thanks for putting him in a good mood,' said Louise as she got ready to leave. 'He's been wearing the carpet out in here this last half-hour.'

'Yeah, sorry, Lou. I completely forgot about it. Anyway you know what he's like, he'll be fine tomorrow.'

In George's rush to commandeer my car I had forgotten that I was due to give a talk to Edgecombe Young Farmers that evening. This was doubly irritating as I didn't want to go anyway. It had been George who had landed me in it.

'It's important for a man in your position to be able to address an audience,' he had said with authority. 'And as an agent at Rumshott you'll often be asked.' I noticed that he never accepted invitations to give a talk but I refrained from arguing the point with him.

'Sophie, could you do something for me?' I ventured carefully.

'Er, what?' she asked raising an eyebrow.

'Give me a lift to Edgecombe this evening.'

'Oh, James, that's miles away. I thought we were having supper at yours tonight.'

'We were but I'd forgotten about this. It'll only take an hour. Please – and I'll take you out to the Green Pepper afterwards as payment!'

Bribery won and by seven o'clock we were wedged in Sophie's mini en route to Edgecombe. This was the first talk I had been asked to give and despite George's assurances that the draft I had prepared was of the highest calibre, I was nervous. I imagined the hall crammed with a hundred or more people all ready to question the validity of what I was saying. What if I had to answer difficult questions or simply lost my voice? I would look a complete fool in front of a great number of Russetshire farmers and might ruin my promising career. By the time we had covered the twenty miles to Edgecombe I was quite rigid with fear and cursed George and his pompous nonsense about public speaking.

The talk was being held in a village hall outside the town centre and we arrived punctually at the appointed time, crunching loudly over the gravel car park to the entrance door. Nervously I gathered my notes and waited for Sophie to lock the car, bracing myself for the hordes of people waiting for my great oration.

'Good luck,' she whispered as I pushed open the door. With my stomach churning wildly and a tremor in my voice we went in to confront my audience.

All four people turned to look at me. Momentarily taken aback I thought that we had come to the wrong meeting until a stout fairhaired chap came forward and asked, 'You James Aden then?'

'Yes, that's right. Am I a bit early?'

'No, no. You're bang on time. I'm afraid we're a bit thin on numbers tonight though. Hope you don't mind.'

'Oh, I see,' I said lamely. 'Um, do you still want me to go ahead?'

'Oh, definitely, if you will,' he enthused. 'Should be well interesting hearing 'bout all the toffs and that.'

He had the local dialect of many Russetshire farmers and I suspected he was a farmer's son who had left school to work on the farm. As my talk was to be about land agency and not estate gossip, I thought he was going to be disappointed.

I suggested we removed the lectern and glass of water from the stage and sit in a little circle in order to make the event less formal. To some extent it worked but I left afterwards with the conclusion that it may well be more daunting to address a hundred or more people but certainly less embarrassing.

Matters were not any less fraught the following morning when Lou put through a call from George.

'Your bloody car's run out of petrol,' he said angrily. 'Why the hell didn't you tell me it was empty?'

'I did try last night but you'd disappeared. I'm sorry but I'd hoped you'd have enough.'

'Well, there obviously isn't. Can you get a Land Rover and come and get me straightaway, please. I've got a meeting at around.'

'Okay, where are you?'

'I'm standing in a pool of pee in the telephone kiosk at Chapel Piddlington.'

Fortunately there was a petrol pump in the stableyard for the estate vehicles so I filled a can and backed the estate Land Rover out of the garage and drove quickly to Piddlington.

George had worked himself up into a state again thanks to my misdemeanours and I reflected that there had been quite a few of these recently. He didn't speak to me when I arrived, he just jumped in the Land Rover and sped away, leaving me to sort out the car.

Luckily I had a string of appointments on the estate all day and was able to keep out of his way until the evening. When I returned at six o'clock, I found him once again pacing around the hall wearing out the carpet.

'Do you realise my blasted car is still at the garage?'

'Oh,' I said, the thought suddenly occurring that maybe this was something to do with me again. 'What's the matter with it now?'

'There's nothing the bloody matter with it. It's what's the bloody matter with you. Don't you want me to get it back? Perhaps you don't like driving in Russet. Is that it?'

'No, no. I am really sorry, George. I didn't realise you'd need me to give you a lift.'

'I shall get Louise to take me there tomorrow morning so would you be so kind as to give me a lift home tonight. Would that be too much of an imposition?' he asked sarcastically.

A tense journey followed as I swiftly returned him home and apart from muttering something about having enough petrol to get him there, he didn't utter a sound.

## Chapter 28

I began to seem that no matter what mode of transport I chose, it would get me into trouble. I had started riding Grehan again to the office some mornings, an extremely civilised and healthy method of conveying myself to work. Lord Leghorn thoroughly approved of the idea and urged me to ride around the park, saying how he loved to see a horse about the place.

'V-very good t-thing, seeing one of my agents on a h-horse,' he said not explaining why he thought that. 'Marvellous p-park to ride in.'

Consequently I often travelled by horse to visit various areas of the estate, the justification being that it was quicker than walking and more ecologically sound than driving. The workmen had grown accustomed to it and Hawthorne was under instructions to keep a stable ready next to the office.

It was Lady Leghorn who found it difficult to comprehend that it was not unusual to find a horse in a stableyard. Admittedly the rest of the stables now formed the estate office and her ladyship's tearoom but there was still a range of unconverted stables. It was a pity not to use them but whenever Grehan appeared, there would, according to her ladyship, be a sudden and rapid increase in the number of flies in her teashop and a terrible stench of horse manure. It was absolute nonsense but she developed an irritating passion for horse-based complaints and I felt it was only a matter of time before she would think of referring it to some bureaucratic health office and have Grehan evicted. After all, it seemed as though local government officers got involved in nearly everything else we did on the estate.

This was particularly the case when managing the let cottages. When alterations or modernisation schemes for the houses were planned these

238

people had control over planning consents and building work. As time progressed they appeared to be given more and more powers and if one considered the regulations set by the electricity board, gas board, water suppliers and drainage authority there ended up being a lot of forms to fill. The strange thing was that all the people I dealt with seemed exactly the same. It made no difference whether I was working on a scheme at Rumshott or on the Gloucestershire estate or in Norfolk. They drove the same model of car, spoke with the same accent and most irritatingly of all, had the same ability to stick rigidly to the regulations irrespective of the individual case.

By far the biggest headache was Rumshott House itself. A Grade I building of national, historical and architectural importance it was subject to just about every control imaginable. Although George rather overemphasised it when he told his lordship that he couldn't fart without listed building consent, he wasn't far off the truth.

Bureaucracy crept into almost every aspect of estate management and even out in the depths of the woods, miles away from anyone, its tentacles penetrated the most innocuous subjects. Trees were planted and felled only with Forestry Commission approval; certain flowers were protected by law and any woodland work had to comply with whatever regulations decreed. Chunks of land were declared Sites of Special Scientific Interest, which meant that there were strict rules over what could and could not be done. Generally, however, these stipulations were sensible and we supported their purpose, which was to protect the country's heritage. Without these rules rare and interesting species of plants and animals might disappear with the loss of their natural habitats. The countryside bureaucrats were different to the building inspectors, being much more willing to listen and discuss ways of solving a problem to everyone's satisfaction. As a result, they had a positive influence on the estate's conservation policy. They offered constructive ideas for the creation of features in the countryside – a new wood perhaps, some more hedges, the restoration of a pond or the planting of an avenue.

Avenues had traditionally been built on the formal approaches to mansion houses, often to mark the celebration of an important event. His lordship had instigated an oak avenue in Rumshott Park to celebrate the births of his grandchildren. Gradually the avenue lengthened as his family grew and a little ceremony would take place each time another tree was planted. As Princess of Arnhustein, Davina might be handed the silver spade kept especially for these occasions, and asked to place the soil over the tree's roots while the family and a few members of staff looked on. Her presence gave any private occasion like that an edge over most other family gatherings.

Like his lordship, I also had a passion for avenues and was lucky that Harbottle Grange boasted a mature lime avenue, lining the half-mile of front drive. It would have been easy to take the surroundings for granted but I never failed to appreciate my own avenue. Even driving up and down it several times a day I marvelled at its stature and reflected on the foresight of the person who had planted it two hundred years earlier. I kept the verges mown and trimmed the suckers off the base of the trees, enjoying the chance to give it some personal attention.

It also became the focus of somebody else's attention, notably on Friday and Saturday nights. Reluctantly I came to the conclusion that this attention wasn't caused by admiration for the magnificence of the avenue but by a much more fundamental pastime. I began to notice the regular appearance of used condoms and scrunched up tissues on my manicured verges. I set about trying to catch the culprits, spending my evenings creeping around in the dark, stumbling over tree roots, treading in sheep droppings and generally working myself into a state. This carried on for several weeks, by which time I was getting rather despondent as I had never even caught a glimpse of the suspects. At one point I even began to wonder whether they were perched in the trees out of sight. Bar sitting up there all night I felt that I had tried everything I could and was reciting my tale of woe at a dinner party one Saturday night at Harbottle when one of the guests ventured to go and have a look for himself.

He had been gone for quite a while when suddenly he burst back into the dining room and threw a bunch of keys on the table.

'There are some people at the back door to see you,' he said with excitement.

I picked up the keys. 'Are these what I think

they are?' I asked him, amazed.

'Yeah, come on.'

I found a young couple about my own age waiting in the yard. The girl was sobbing profusely on her boyfriend's arm while he stood ashen faced and terrified under the yard's bright floodlight.

I think I was more surprised than they were and I noticed with some caution that this bloke could have laid me out easily. He was twice my size and rather thuggish looking. Quite why he was so frightened I didn't know but clearly he was regretting his misuse of my avenue.

It was the girl's sobbing that made me take pity on them. I reflected that it couldn't be much fun confining one's sex life to the back seat of a car. I gave the keys back, saying that if they insisted upon having sex in my driveway then they could at least remove the evidence. I don't believe they ever returned but suspected that treelined avenues would remain forever stamped in their minds.

## Chapter 29

I sometimes wondered what particular events or places were special to Lord and Lady Leghorn. They lived in such splendour and luxury that, what for most people might be something to cherish, to them was just ordinary. Her ladyship would charter a private jet to fly her to Paris for a spot of clothes shopping without a second's thought. Fenella would go on ahead with the luggage and be waiting at the Ritz for her ladyship's arrival. It was a very different lifestyle.

I know that one of his lordship's great memories occurred on the day that Lady Davina announced her engagement to His Royal Highness The Prince of Arnhustein. The Leghorns mingled with the crowds of wellwishers outside the Arnhustein Palace, no doubt aware that from that day onwards everything was going to change. Due to the fame and importance of the Royal Family of Arnhustein, the future of the Leghorns and Rumshott also altered. Although already a prominent and aristocratic family with wealth of their own, this connection hugely increased their significance. The connections led to a life of great interest but inevitably much of the public and media attention was unwanted, especially when private concerns were twisted by journalists to provide more exciting news.

It became impossible for Lady Davina to nip back to Rumshott in her car for a quiet weekend. Every visit had to be planned and carefully coordinated with the police and the Royal Protection Service. As Her Royal Highness The Princess of Arnhustein she became a closely guarded member of their Royal Family and a single night's stay at Rumshott involved huge preparation. A day or two in advance of her visit the police would arrive, set up temporary headquarters in the estate office and seal off the park. The massive ornate wrought-iron gates at the East and West lodges would be manned by policemen who would only admit those with security passes. Sniffer dogs would check drains and culverts, exploring every nook and cranny of the house and stableyard, while other areas would be sealed off with special tape. Marksmen would patrol the park boundaries and a sinister looking van bristling with aerials would identify locations where a sniper might hide.

Presumably the police felt that these precautions were necessary although at Rumshott there were never any particular threats against Davina's safety. Unless that was, you talked to PC Cripps who was under the illusion that Carlos the Jackal made frequent visits to the park. I spotted the alleged Jackal one day cycling through the park and determined that in truth he was a frail, elderly pensioner doing all he could to cycle the two miles from his home and back again.

An unhappy coincidence occurred one Friday afternoon which ruined my progress on an insurance revaluation. I had called in to see Viscount Rumshott at the Folly, his secluded house in the park, about some new gates he wanted. Swearing me to absolute secrecy, he told me that the princess would be staying there at the weekend, unbeknown to anyone. She wanted a complete break from the constraints of her royal life and where better to hide than her brother's secure house at Rumshott. Not even the Leghorns knew she was visiting so I promised him my silence and put it out of my mind. This was fine until I returned to the office and found Stan Cripps gossiping in the hall with Louise.

'Everything all right, Stan?' I asked.

'Can't complain, James,' he replied. 'Nothing

much going on in any of your villages at the moment.'

'Good, that's what we want to hear. Lou, can you see to these for me please. They've got to go out tonight,' I said handing her some envelopes.

'Just seen Carlos in the park,' Stan added.

'Oh. What was he doing here?'

'Usual. Looking for HRH.'

'I am sure you make all this up, Stan. He's a harmless old man out for a cycle ride. Not some assassin as you seem to think.'

'Well, you never know,' he said darkly, 'there's many been fooled by what they see.'

'It's a lot of nonsense – for a start where do you suppose he keeps his rifle? You can see it's not strapped to the cross bar!'

He did not appreciate my flippancy and I left him to persuade Louise of his convictions. It was a particularly annoying sighting though because although I felt he was wrong, the coincidence made me a little uneasy. What if something un- toward happened? I had been sworn to secrecy by Viscount Rumshott so I couldn't discuss it with anyone else. I was going through the altern- atives in my mind when Cripps' police car roared up outside my office window. I had presumed that he was still in the hall but he had apparently gone off on one of his wanders around the estate and with desperately unfortunate timing had met the princess driving in.

'What the bloody hell's the princess doing 'ere,' he asked in a panic. 'I haven't been told anything about it.' Under normal procedure the Russet- shire Constabulary were advised of her visits and

Stan would be warned by his superiors.

'Stan, come into my office a moment, would you?' I closed the door behind him. 'She's here on a private visit, totally secret. Staying at the Folly. Nobody's supposed to know apart from one or two of her personal protection team. Certainly nobody at Russet HQ, which is why you haven't been told.'

He looked surprised. 'Is that normal?' he asked.

'No, it's not but it's really nothing to do with us so I'd be grateful if you'd keep quiet about it.'

He was a conscientious policeman and the situation bothered him, especially having seen Carlos earlier. A long, heated discussion followed and although I asked him to forget about the matter I suspect he reported it to someone more senior. Whatever he did he managed to maintain secrecy and we did not witness any extra police activity during the weekend.

The secrecy reminded me of the Harwoods, tenant farmers over on the Little Washbury estate in Gloucestershire, with whom I had an appointment during the week. The Harwoods had been Leghorn tenants for centuries and were a very private, secretive family who never raised their voices. In fact it went further than that – they always whispered.

Most of the farmers I came across were, on the whole, a pretty hearty lot with voices to match. A necessity when shouting at their stubborn animals or cussing some machine that wouldn't work. But at the Harwoods' place a serene tranquillity prevailed. Mr and Mrs Harwood ran the farm with the help of their four children, three boys and a girl. Despite being in their fifties the children were all unmarried. The whole family lived together in apparent harmony in the large farmhouse and divided their responsibilities in a traditional manner. Mrs Harwood kept the house, Miss Harwood cared for the calves and poultry and the men did everything else. It was a good mixed farm with arable land, cattle, sheep and a few pigs and must have been pretty much self-sufficient with its substantial kitchen garden behind the house. I doubted they had ever experienced shopping trolleys with wobbly wheels or checkout girls asking if they wanted cash back.

Miss Harwood had attended a week's course in bookkeeping some thirty years earlier and being the only member of the family to have gone on to further education, as they put it, was also the family administrator. Three or four times a year she would telephone the estate office to make an appointment for me to visit.

'Harwood of Little Washbury,' she would whisper from the black Bakelite handset in the farmhouse kitchen. I could envisage her crouched over the oak roll top desk stacked with a mountain of papers.

She was difficult to hear but the appointment would be made and in due course I would visit the farm. The procedure never varied and followed the same lines as a royal visit. The Harwood men would be waiting for me in the yard, standing in a line like a row of soldiers on parade wearing what I suppose must have been suits in an earlier life. As they opted for black or grey city suits, tweed trilbies and heavy hobnailed boots I could never decide whether they were going for a business or country look. We would then have a tour of the farmyard, Mr Harwood leading the way, then me, then the brothers in descending order of age. We would inspect the buildings and the animals inside. Not a lot was said and only when we all clustered around in a tight group was it possible to hear. It was all very peaceful and the sudden call of a blackbird was enough to make us all start in alarm.

Eventually we would progress towards the house via a long stone-flagged path that edged around a murky duck pond and through a door in an ancient brick wall hidden under a magnificent clematis.

The Harwood ladies would be waiting in the kitchen with a sumptuous tea laid out on an enormous scrubbed pine table. We would sit there in silence, eating the array of home-made bread, cheese, eggs, ham, cakes and bottled fruit, nodding and smiling across the table. The scene was bizarre as the men in their illassorted suits resembled a Mafia gang plotting a raid.

After tea there would be a collective intake of breath as Miss Harwood stood up and moved over to the writing desk. Whispering through an agenda the business matters would be discussed, decisions taken and noted on a little piece of paper which was then placed next to an anti-quated mahogany wireless set on the dresser. These were the most civilised meetings I ever conducted on estate business and apart from the time I had terrible hay fever and my sneezing sent shock waves through the entire family, were the quietest moments that I ever spent outside a library.

Strangely enough, it was a combination of silence and concealment which led to one of the most uncivilised meetings I ever had in the estate office. Mrs Nethergate, the churchwarden of St Peter's in Great Bassett, had come in to see me about some restoration work which was needed in the Leghorns' private chapel. She stood stout and solid in the reception hall as I went out to greet her. I ushered her tweed-clad figure into my office where she seated her substantial bottom on a fine oak Windsor chair in front of my desk. She was a stickler for punctuality and correctness and by all accounts ruled the church with a ferocity that even the vicar found overwhelming. She was not a lover of dogs and with no canine attractions about her, Bramble remained half asleep, hidden under the massive partner's desk. In fact I had quite forgotten she was there until this nauseous enveloping stench came drifting over me as I listened to Mrs Nethergate's crisp educated voice decreeing what should or shouldn't be done to the chapel. In vain I hoped that the smell would somehow come to a halt some way from Mrs Nethergate but I soon realised by the look of alarm on her heavily powdered, bespectacled face that it had not. Of course a lady in her position had to feign indifference and she ploughed on relentlessly, but the glare in her eyes said it all. She thought it was me. I hadn't had the chance to explain that the dog was the cause of our discomfort when there was the unmistakable sound of a loud fart and another wave of rotten odour engulfed the desk.

It was too much for Mrs Nethergate and with a righteous gathering of her handbag, her pearl necklace clinking in annoyance, she stood up abruptly and marched out of my office, saying, 'Mr Aden, your manners are simply disgusting.'

I was so startled by the swiftness of her departure that I was unable to retrieve the situation and from then on Mrs Nethergate conducted our discussions over the telephone. Worse still, and I believe showing a lack of Christian understanding, she took to sitting on a pew on the opposite side of the church from me.

I was the only representative from the estate who regularly attended services at Great Bassett. I suppose the attraction of many village churches is unclear to most – they are cold, the congregation elderly and the format of the services stilted. Although attendance is clearly in decline this is not for the lack of trying, as there are many ministers who strive continuously and with great enthusiasm to spread the word. Bassett was fortunate to have such an incumbent. The Reverend Tim Postlethwaite was a short bald man reminiscent of Friar Tuck. He attended to his parishes with abundant energy, ministering to the sick and lonely irrespective of their beliefs. He acted with deference to the earl and with compliance to Mrs Nethergate and her worthies but above all he appeared to have a faith that God was always with him.

This was brought home to me, not from the pulpit in the beautiful church of St Peter's but in a self-service petrol station on the Russet bypass.

I had stopped to fill up my car with petrol when the vicar drew up alongside, his green Morris Minor grating to a shuddering halt. It was a particularly windy day and two facts stuck in my mind. As his cassock blew high in the wind it revealed a most extraordinary pair of pink flowery ladies' trousers and the cigarette firmly wedged in his mouth sent showers of sparks like confetti over the petrol station forecourt. I thought then that if a man could stand in a petrol station wearing a pair of pink ladies' trousers while filling his car with petrol as sparks fell all around him, he must have an unshakeable faith in someone above.

## Chapter 30

I had flu. One minute my teeth were chattering with cold, the next I was sweating profusely. Every bone and muscle in my body ached and even regular doses of painkiller didn't do much to relieve it. I had rung the office to be greeted by George's usual comment of, 'Well, I hope it's not trivial,' and then been passed on to Sophie who had more helpfully offered to come down after work to make some supper and feed the animals.

The morning dawned to a cold winter's day. There had been a hard frost during the night and it was snowing – a fine snow, as though the fields were being dusted with a coat of icing sugar.

Most of the sheep were in the field in front of the house and I could hear them bleating plaintively for their feed. The grass, white, frozen and unpalatable, held no attraction for them. I struggled into some old clothes, my head spinning as if I was slightly drunk and with a horrible racking cough I crept downstairs.

I took my dogs, Bramble and Jess, with me and they sniffed around, no doubt searching for rats whilst I fed Grehan, changed her rugs and turned her out in the field. Then I began on the sheep. Bales of hay and sheep feed had to be stacked into the trailer before I could climb on to the tractor. As soon as the ewes heard the engine they set up a deafening chorus of bleating, knowing breakfast was on its way. There were three lots of sheep, the rams in one paddock, some late finishing lambs in another and the main breeding flock by the house. It was easiest and least frustrating to feed the smaller lots first and then brave the mass of three hundred ewes who seemed intent on throwing themselves under the tractor. Feeling short tempered because of the flu, I drove slowly through the heaving carpet of woolly backs towards the feed troughs. Jess, my collie sheepdog, ran alongside trying to clear a path but she was inclined to single out one ewe at a time so leaving two hundred and ninety nine in danger of falling under the tyres. It got worse when I emptied the sacks of feed into the troughs as the manic rush would lift me off my feet. It was difficult to manage feeling as I did but the job got done.

Most of the time I loved having the farm and it

made an interesting change from the daily routine and problems of the estate. Not that the farm didn't have its own problems, the most serious being that I had bought the wrong type of sheep. At the time I had bought some ewes that I believed were good value for money and would get me off to a promising start at Harbottle. The hundred Beulah speckled-face ewes were attractive looking sheep and also fairly small, important if I was going to handle them on my own. They might have been small but they were anything but easy to handle. In fact they were wild. Worse still, they had Houdini tendencies and could escape from any enclosure. The farm was well fenced but if there was even the smallest hole somewhere, they would find it and make a dash for my neighbour's corn. The occasional foray was acceptable and the adjoining farmers were good enough about it but eventually the sheep became marauding pests and little groups of them would disappear only to surface on a distant farm. Locally they became known as the Flying Beulahs and over a period of time their numbers began to dwindle. I realised that this was not a profitable way to keep sheep when I found some being sold in Russet market one Saturday. The irate farmer selling them knew they were mine but there was no way I could prove it.

Despite the dwindling numbers most of the farms in the area eventually had a visit from them but for some unfortunate reason they particularly decided to plague Richard Sparkes, an estate farmer at Little Bassett. He had been vehemently against my occupation of Harbottle Grange

Farm, mistakenly believing that it would otherwise have been added to his tenancy.

One afternoon when the Flying Beulahs really were flying, I met him at his farmhouse to discuss the partial re-roofing of one wing where rain was seeping in along a valley gutter. I was just leaving when he said, 'Why don't you keep your bloody sheep in?'

I hadn't realised any were out and said so.

'Well what the hell are these?' he continued, leading me over to a stable in the corner of the yard.

I peered in over the half-door and recognised six of my Beulahs standing there.

'Oh, dear,' I exclaimed apologetically. 'Yes they're mine I'm afraid.'

'Bloody right they're yours.'

'Um, well I'll come over after work with the Land Rover and fetch them if that's okay with you Richard.'

'You'll have to do better 'an that. I need the stable. You can put 'em in your car and take 'em now.'

'In my car,' I repeated in horror at the thought of six sheep in the back of my Golf GTI.

'Come on, I'll help ye,' he said with a sadistically cheerful tone in his voice. Without having a flaming row there wasn't anything I could do except load them in. Of course, being Beulahs it was not as easy as that. Once we had got one in it would leap out as we tried to get the second in. This went on amidst much swearing from Mr Sparkes and some rather hurtful comments about land agents pretending to be farmers. At last they were all loaded, including one wedged in the foot well of the passenger seat which bleated painfully loudly in my ear as I drove them home while the rest of them crapped all over my car.

Mr Sparkes was rather short sighted in having the last laugh over that meeting because he was not the only tenant needing repairs. There was always a long list of requests to do this or that and I spent a fair proportion of my time inspecting the problems. In theory we dealt with these things on a first-come first-served basis unless something really urgent came along. Occasionally if one of the tenants was being unnecessarily awkward then we'd shove them to the bottom of the list and every minute I spent cleaning sheep droppings out of my car Mr Sparkes' roofing got further and further away.

By six o'clock in the evening on the day I had flu I was feeling feverish and was delighted when Sophie arrived armed with honey, lemons and a bottle of whisky.

'Am I glad to see you,' I croaked. 'I feel absolutely awful. Haven't been able to do anything all day.'

'Oh, poor you. I'll try and sort some things out for you. Do you want a drink? Hot lemon and whisky?'

She disappeared off to the kitchen whilst I lay aching and shivering in my bed. It was an effort to sit up and take the hot drink from her but gradually the whisky started to take effect.

She disappeared off downstairs again and I snuggled down under the covers luxuriating in the warmth and the comfort of knowing she was there. My peace was disturbed by Sophie shouting up the stairs, 'James, there's a man at the back door wanting to get his caravan out.'

Oh, Lord, that's one of the last people I want to see I thought to myself. In my feverish state I had forgotten that Mr Hinds had rung earlier.

'Okay, I'll have to come down. Tell him to hold on a minute while I get some clothes on,' I called back. Mr Hinds was a customer of an enterprise that I ran and considered an act of social responsibility. I stored caravans, about fifty of them, in an immense unused building on the farm, believing that the only place a caravan should be was out of sight. 'Sorry to have kept you waiting, Mr Hinds,' I said, greeting him at the back door. 'I've been in bed all day with flu.'

He took a step backwards at this news and with a nasal twang assured me that he wouldn't get too near for fear of catching it himself.

When we arrived at the barn it was obvious that Mr Hinds had attempted to back the caravan out of the barn. One thing I had discovered early on was that most caravan owners were incapable of reversing. No amount of mirrors or other gadgetry mounted on their cars seemed to make the slightest difference and I had spent many frustrated moments waiting while they attempted the impossible. I was used to backing farm trailers and so it was usually easier to jump in their cars and do the job myself but on this occasion, Mr Hinds obviously thought that I would infect his car with the flu germ and insisted upon fiddling about on his own. It was hopeless and eventually

256

I persuaded him to unhook it and with some effort we pushed it out of the barn.

'What do you want me to do with the animals?' Sophie asked when I returned.

'Could you do the dogs and Grehan for me, please. I've rung Tom Dagg, he's looking after the sheep for a few days. I've just got to write down what's to be done and get you to leave the note in the feed shed on the window sill.'

Once the animals were sorted out Sophie made some supper. We ate in my bedroom, listening vaguely to a man on the radio talking about edible mushrooms, and I felt a sense of closeness to Sophie and gratitude for her coming to help me out. She sat beside me on the bed and I put my arm around her shoulders.

'Thanks for coming over and putting up with an invalid,' I said.

'Don't worry, it's no problem. I didn't have anything else to do anyway.'

'Well, don't sit around getting bored, go downstairs, if you want.'

'Yeah, I'll go and light a fire in the drawing room and watch some television if you're sure you don't mind.'

'Course I don't. I'll just go off to sleep anyway. Are you staying the night?'

'Yup, I've brought my stuff but I'm not going to sleep in here.'

'That doesn't surprise me. I think the bed in the nursery is made up. I should go there, it's warmer.'

To my relief, she stayed for several days, coping brilliantly with dogs, horse and me while I stayed pathetically under my duvet.

# Chapter 31

The following week I was back in my office catching up with my work when the phone rang.

'It's his lordship for you, James,' said Louise.

'Thanks.' There was a flurry of clicking sounds, a distant 'hello' and then the dialling tone. I buzzed Lou's extension.

'Where's he gone? I think you've cut him off.'

'Oh God, have I?' she exclaimed. 'I'll try and get him back.'

This sometimes happened when Louise got flustered and pushed the wrong button, or it might occur at the other end if Lady Leghorn walked into his lordship's study and he would drop the phone like a naughty schoolboy, accidentally cutting off his call.

'His lordship again.'

'Morning, Lord Leghorn,' I said loudly in case it went dead again.

'Ah, m-morning, James,' he replied. 'I've g-got an item for the next m-management agenda, please,' he continued. 'Plumbing.'

'Plumbing, my lord?' I hadn't heard anything about this before.

'Yes – p-plumbing. Please put it on the agenda. Goodbye.'

This sounded like a Lady Leghorn idea and by the shortness of the conversation I suspected that she was with him when he rang.

The regular fortnightly meetings attended by his lordship, George and myself were preceded by an agenda and no sooner had George received his from Louise the following morning, than he rang me.

'What the hell is item four?' he barked.

'Plumbing,' I replied.

'I can see that,' he said, 'I can read. What does it mean?'

'I haven't got a clue. His lordship rang yesterday and asked me to put it down. Didn't explain anything.'

'Bugger. He's on to some hare-brained scheme by the sound of it. Or more likely she is. See if you can find anything out before the meeting will you. Forewarned forearmed and all that.'

It did not take long. Later that afternoon her ladyship rang.

'James, WHERE IS TIM KNIGHT?' she screamed. I held the earpiece away before replying.

'I believe he's working at Bassett today, Lady Leghorn. We're having some problems with...' She cut across my answer.

'He is MY PLUMBER and he should be HERE in the house. WHAT is the point of employing a plumber if whenever I need him he's in somebody else's house? How can I run this place for his lordship without help? FROM NOW ON HE ONLY WORKS IN THIS HOUSE. DO YOU UNDERSTAND?'

Crash, down went the receiver. Wearily I put my head in my hands and thought, here we go again. We hadn't had one of her ladyship's 'things' for a

259

while and I had relished the calm between the storms. The stress she caused if she was feeling neglected was immeasurable for all those she dragged into whatever scheme she was hatching.

Of course she was being unreasonable. She knew that as well as I did but that didn't make the slightest difference once the momentum began. Tim Knight, a resolutely patient man with an intricate knowledge of Rumshott House and all its pipes, boilers and drains was one of the only men who could come out of one of her ladyship's interviews and laugh. He would shake his head in despair, explain that her orders were impossible, ill-thought out or plainly insane and have a good chuckle before settling down to a sandwich and his *Daily Telegraph* while he pondered what to do.

We had suffered a similar outburst six months earlier and I had reached an agreement with Lady Leghorn that Tim would report directly to the house each morning to deal with any problems first before going out on the estate. As for being her plumber – the estate paid his wages because he was employed to work on the estate, not solely in the house. Not that that made the slightest difference.

Anyway, this was obviously something to do with item four on the agenda and I went up to George's office to report. 'Well, we can cope with that,' he said. 'We'll just emphasise the fact that he's at Rumshott first and then on the estate. It'll blow over – I expect she's got a tap that needs fixing and he wasn't there to do it instantly.

Sadly there turned out to be more to it than

just a tap and the following management meeting took a turn for the worse when we reached item four.

'Item four, my lord, plumbing,' I read out from my little upright chair. 'Something you asked to be included.'

His lordship twitched slightly and rearranged himself in the deep recesses of the feather cushions, placed his fountain pen on the Hepplewhite table beside him and looked worried. I glanced at George who was already gearing himself up for an argument, his eyes unblinking and aggressive, his face reddening and fingers clasped tightly around his inhaler.

'Ah, yes. N-number f-four,' his lordship continued as though he had forgotten it was listed. 'Plumbing.'

I'd already said that and as he dithered I could almost feel the heat emitting from George's chair. If we didn't get on with this quickly I feared he would go off like a missile and hit the ornate plaster ceiling just to the left of the French crystal chandelier giving us yet another building repair to sort out.

'I w-want to h-have the h-house r-re-plumbed,' he said.

There was an eerie silence. I dared not look at either of them but I detected a small movement from George's chair. The early eighteenth-century bracket clock on the mantelpiece continued to prove that time still passed and a man with a horse stared disinterestedly from the Stubbs painting above the sofa.

'Do what, my lord?' George exploded, so loudly

261

that both his lordship and I started in our seats.

'R-re-plumb the house,' he repeated calmly as though we were talking about some 25-milli-metre copper pipe and a couple of taps.

Another silence followed, broken by a gasp on George's inhaler.

'What on earth do you want to do that for, my lord?' he questioned.

'Well I d-don't t-think it's been d-done for a long t-time,' Lord Leghorn replied. 'I suspect most of it is Victorian in fact.'

'I suspect most of it is,' confirmed George, 'but what's wrong with it? Are there any particular problems?' He looked at me.

'No, not that I'm aware of. Are there any, my lord?' I asked.

'N-no, n-nothing wrong really. B-but we must keep up to date with these things. D-don't want to burden Edward with a l-liability of a house.'

This was ridiculous. The family trusts meant that Edward could far more easily afford to re-plumb the place when it needed doing and in any case this was a Lady Leghorn idea and she was unlikely to be interested in Edward's liabilities.

His lordship continued, 'Of course, w-while we're at it we'll r-redo the heating as well.'

George nearly fell off his seat. 'My lord,' he yelped and took another puff on his inhaler, 'do you realise what this will involve?'

'Yes, but w-while we've g-got Tim K-Knight it'll give him something t-to do.'

'I'm sorry, my lord, but he's got far too much to do as it is and he couldn't possibly undertake this kind of job, we'd have to engage a specialist firm.

He couldn't physically cope if he worked here the rest of his life. It's a huge project.'

There were literally miles of pipes within the house, forming a bewildering maze of metalwork hidden behind, beneath and above floors, walls and ceilings. The boilers alone, immense great monsters that guzzled oil and were powerful enough to run an ocean liner, occupied vast sections of the cellars. This had to be one of her ladyship's most insane ideas yet and I could see item five on the agenda was a long way off.

Very eloquently and at great length, George set about sabotaging the plan. He was practised at doing so and mentioned the upheaval, the re-decoration, the mess and the cost. None of these had been considered. Where was the money coming from he asked. They would need perhaps a million pounds and really all for Edward's benefit – did they really want all the aggravation and expense on his behalf?

He glanced at me. I nodded imperceptibly. That should do the trick I thought. If his lordship repeated the conversation verbatim back to her ladyship, those final words would be the sentence of death to the project. She was not known for spending large amounts of money for the benefit of her stepchildren.

It had been a costly hour or two with the Ventolin inhaler but with a sense of relief it seemed likely that the immediate drama might be over. What we had to watch for now was her ladyship's replacement idea – she was bound to see this as a victory for the estate and launch a counter attack.

Surprisingly no immediate retaliation surfaced. No tantrums, no recriminations to the office, nothing. It did not feel right, something was missing, the air of tension that hung over Rumshott seemed to have gone. Her ladyship's energy and lordship's money had to be channelled somewhere and it wasn't obvious where. An ambush seemed the most likely choice.

It was a subtle plan, as I found out gradually. Over a period of several weeks I kept coming across an assortment of men scurrying around Rumshott House saying things like, 'The purple and gold would be absolutely divine, darling,' or, 'We simply must have pink orchids in her ladyship's boudoir, sweetie,' which indicated to me that some London designers were at work. Then I noticed some Louis XV chairs had been re-gilded, a few paintings restored and some objets d'art purchased. Lady Leghorn was back on track with a restoration project. I kept out of the way – anything was better than the re-plumbing scenario.

Amongst his duties as plumber, Tim Knight had the dubious honour of being in charge of the Leghorn flag, which was flown proudly from the most prominent part of the roof, high above the front entrance. He had asked me to go up there with him so that he could show me what to do if ever the flag needed raising in his absence. Rumshott's roof, in common with most stately homes, was predominantly flat and covered in acres and acres of lead. Hidden behind the parapet walls and accessed by a myriad of wooden walkways and small ladders it formed a sunbathing trap of sheer perfection. We climbed up there one hot afternoon and I was teetering on the edge marvelling at the view of the park and the contours of the hills when I was abruptly startled by the unexpected view of three shapely pairs of girls' breasts. The opportunity to admire a different set of contours did not last long as three coloured towels swiftly appeared amidst panicky squeals. We had disturbed some of the house staff in their private hideaway.

## Chapter 32

'Ladies and gentlemen, please welcome our guest speaker this evening, the divisional president of the Royal Institution of Chartered Surveyors.' A long round of applause followed as a well built, ruddy-faced man wearing a tweed suit climbed on to the podium.

Looking around the conference hall I noticed that the majority of the audience were also in the uniform of the rural practice surveyor or land agent: tweed jacket, Viyella tattersall checked shirt, moleskin trousers and polished brogues. The president began speaking – something to do with encouraging more people into the profession – but my mind soon started to wander, reflecting on how I had arrived at my position as a resident agent.

Isolated and immersed in the running of Rumshott it was easy to forget that I had trained as a chartered surveyor. I spent so much time engaged in the trivial matters of repairs, distressed tenants and the demanding Leghorns that my training seemed only vaguely connected with my work. Most of the other people in the room would be based in offices in local towns and have a multitude of clients. Their clients would be farmers or maybe small landowners who had no need for the full-time assistance of one or more land agents.

The resident land agents dotted about the room were in a different boat and, strangely, considered themselves the elite of the profession. I could never understand that because we were the ones most likely to be sticking our heads down manholes detecting why a sewer was blocked or ferreting about in some damp cottage looking for leaking pipes. Perhaps it was the cachet of working for the aristocracy on their great landed estates that had a lot to do with it. Anyway, it was important to venture out to these meetings occasionally and mix with colleagues and be seen to have some interest in the organisation that represented us. George and Sophie were both there making it a little office outing although George had arrived earlier as he held a position on the committee. He sat bristling with righteous importance on the stage glaring sternly at those unfortunate enough to cough or emit some other audible offering. He never could explain his exact function on the committee and as far as I was able to ascertain, it merely ensured that he received a free gin and tonic before each meeting.

Sophie had not been keen on attending the event and it was only by tempting her with dinner at the Red Lion that she had agreed to join me. It was a renowned place to eat and although we tended to go out somewhere each week for a meal we hadn't yet been to the Red Lion together. I felt it was particularly necessary to eat a good meal as the previous night she had organised a fondue party at her cottage which was about as exciting as attending an RICS meeting. Both are the sort of events that you have to attend every so often but rather wish you hadn't. Six of us had sat, ravenously hungry, in a circle clustered around a little pot of boiling oil waiting for bits of meat to cook, one at a time. The idea of cooking enough food for half-a-dozen people with an apparatus fired by a single candle seemed ludicrous. I found the five-minute wait between mouthfuls frustrating but the girls took delight in using the available time to gossip. After a couple of hours' hard work and a replacement candle I had consumed the equivalent of a young child's portion when the monotony was relieved by the telephone ringing.

'James, it's George trying to find you,' Sophie said. 'He guessed you might be here.'

'Sorry to disturb your party, James,' he barked, 'but I'm out of the office tomorrow and something's come up that you need to deal with urgently.'

'What's happened?'

'I've just had the organiser of some little outfit called the Walk Where You Want Society on the phone here making complaints about a blocked

267

footpath somewhere on the estate. A lot of tosh in my view but the thing is this. I told her to ring the office in the morning as I was not prepared to discuss it at home so find out what they want and investigate. Just don't promise to do anything.'

'Okay, but why the drama?' I asked.

'Because potentially they could be trouble. She was on about reporting it to the papers. You know what these woolly hat brigade are like – they'll do anything for a bit of publicity.'

I always felt there was an anomaly with these people. The organisations which represented their interests were often aggressive and yet the people that I met on my travels around the estate were the complete opposite. Even the name of the most well-known group, the Ramblers' Association, conveyed a calmness. It was typically English, not hiking or trekking, not even walking. They rambled in a benign and civilised way from teashop to teashop while the more serious members carried rucksacks containing the necessary lifesaving supplies needed for an outing in the Russetshire countryside.

However, I was grateful for the warning, because no sooner had I sat down at my desk the next morning than the telephone rang and a charming sounding lady introduced herself.

'My name is Karen Boodle,' she said, 'from the Walk Where You Want Society.'

She went onto explain that she was investigating the alleged blocking of a footpath on the estate, which contravened the Highways Act. She asked for a map of the estate so as to be absolutely certain of the ownership of the field in question.

'I'm afraid not,' I replied.

'Why not?' she bit back.

'Because we consider that to be confidential information and do not release maps to just anyone who happens to ask for them.'

She became less charming and aggressively threatened to go to the newspapers about it. We often had this sort of nonsense thrown at us because it was an easy and cheap trick to play. Rumshott and Earl Leghorn, as father to the Princess of Arnhustein, were good copy for the tabloids. Miss Boodle knew that, which was without doubt the reason for her targeting that particular path. The Walk Where You Want Society must have needed some high-profile case to advance awareness of the organisation

Displeased with the outcome of our conversation, the short section of path that crossed a field of kale near the estate village of Lower Maplethorpe was duly featured in a newspaper as threatened. PRINCESS'S FATHER STOPS WALKERS and EARL IN FOOTPATH ROW were the kind of tantalising headlines plastered over the front pages.

Unfortunately after the first article was published other reporters started ringing the house wanting to speak to Lord Leghorn who of course didn't know anything about it. I braced myself for the inevitable attack the moment I read the newspaper and sure enough the missiles were launched from the countess' four-poster bed exactly as anticipated. 'I will NOT HAVE his lordship's name dragged through the mud,' she screamed at me.

I could hear the rustle of bedclothes as she squirmed around feverishly between the sheets. How she could manage such an offensive so early in the morning was beyond my imagination but she had only just begun.

'WHY DON'T YOU MANAGE THE BLOODY ESTATE PROPERLY AND AVOID RUINING OUR GOOD NAME?' she shouted.

The blasts kept raining down and the fact that the situation was outside our control evaded her. I never had an opportunity to explain.

'It's ALL your fault. GROSS MISMANAGE-MENT.'

The fact that no one had yet grasped was that the land was let and farmed by a tenant. It was not his lordship's kale that was causing the trouble but everybody became so busy making a terrible fuss that they missed this vital point. Furthermore the land didn't even belong to Lord Leghorn, it was owned by one of the family trusts so when the case eventually went to court, Miss Boodle, who had lodged the case against the earl personally, was forced to withdraw it and make a public apology.

Miss Boodle's bullying tactics ended in embar-rassment for her and a waste of her society's funds. It was a pity that she hadn't tried to discuss the matter more rationally beforehand and I was alarmed to read some time later that she had been appointed to a highranking post with another similar but larger society. No doubt she would be leading an even greater number of woolly hats into confrontation with landowners.

I had only just finished with this commotion

and was hoping for some uninterrupted peace when Hawthorne decided to make a drama out of something which should have been a simple problem. Normally he quietly got on with his tasks and there would be no word from him, just a courteous touch of his cloth cap as he chugged past the window on the lawnmower. Apart from the lawns he was responsible for winding the stableyard clock every Monday morning. It was not a complicated or onerous duty but Hawthorne had a very sensitive nature and the day the minute hand fell off caused him considerable personal distress. I didn't think for one moment that it was his fault but Tim Knight, who happened to be walking underneath and narrowly missed being speared by the brass digit, took great delight in ribbing Hawthorne about it. To get to the winding mechanism it was necessary to follow a series of little rickety stairs and ladders which climbed up into the stableyard tower high above the estate office. Visibly upset by the incident he came into the office to report it to me, knocking tentatively on the door.

'Come in,' I shouted. Nothing happened.

'Come in,' I shouted again, after which I heard some whispering on the far side. Still nothing happened.

Then there was another knock.

'Bloody come in,' I yelled at the top of my voice. This time the door opened slightly and Hawthorne's head appeared.

'Do you think I could see you for a moment?' he asked hesitantly.

'Yes, for goodness' sake, come in. Whatever's

the problem?'

Twitching slightly he held up the minute hand of the clock.

'This,' he explained unclearly.

I peered at it inquisitively, wondering what on earth he had found. I hadn't got a clue what it was.

'Ah, yes,' I said. 'What is it?'

'The bugger's come orf the clock,' he said.

I still did not grasp what he was getting at and bearing in mind that it was bent at a ninety-degree angle after its fall, it was hardly surprising.

'What's come off what clock?' I asked, seeking clarification.

'This clock,' he replied pointing at the ceiling. Conversations with Hawthorne tended to get drawn out because he had a peculiar knack of imparting very little information. Suddenly I caught on.

'Oh, it's a hand off the stableyard clock. I see now. Bit bent. What happened?'

'Fell off.'

'When?'

'Just now.'

'How?'

'Um – don't rightly know.'

I looked at him twisting it around in his hands, waiting for a little more enlightenment.

'Um – just fell off.' He was beginning to sweat and I sensed that his cap was about to be removed, brow wiped with the top of it, then replaced. It was. I also sensed that we weren't going to get very much further with the diagnosis.

'Well never mind, these things happen. I'll ring Smiths of Derby and get them to fix it. Thanks for letting me know.'

Very cautiously, as if I might pounce on him, he tentatively reached forward and deposited the brass object on my desk. After some more hesitating in the doorway he departed. I could never imagine why he got so nervous with me. I knew that he was frightened by George's shouting, which made him jump about like a mouse in a feed sack, but I always felt we could discuss things quite calmly.

Unfortunately that wasn't the end of Hawthorne's drama with the clock. The absence of the minute hand upset the mechanism somehow and its time keeping became erratic. It gained time, lost it, stopped altogether for half a day and, as it was relied on by the estate staff, this caused quite a muddle. Hawthorne took the brunt of the blame well enough until midday on the following Thursday when the lonesome hour hand jammed, causing a continuous striking of the loud bell. Amidst the confusion of some elderly visitors who thought war had broken out, he was roused from his lunchtime snooze in the potting shed and ordered to stop the clock for the first time in living memory.

# Chapter 33

It had long been apparent that Viscount Rumshott's interest in the estate was being thwarted by the Earl's refusal to allow him much significant involvement. Although he would inherit it all one day his father kept a hold on the reins, mainly because of the influence of the Countess. They needed the estate income to provide them with enough money to fund their expensive lifestyle.

It was due to this frustration that Edward came to see me in the estate office with a plan.

'Come in, Edward,' I greeted him, 'it's good to see you. You haven't been down lately for a while.'

'Hello, no, I'm afraid I haven't. Not too many dramas in my absence I hope?'

'Everything's fine at the moment, thanks. I'm sure you'll let me know if there's anything you want done.'

'Well, I've actually come down to talk to you about an idea that I've been working on for a while, partly to gauge your reaction as a land agent and partly because I'll need your help if it goes ahead.'

'I'm intrigued,' I replied, smiling. 'What have you in mind?'

'It's a fairly major investment in fact. But one that I think will be a major asset to the family over the years, though I suspect there'll be some resistance to it at first. Elizabeth and I would like to buy another estate, in the Scottish Highlands.'

I was taken aback. I had thought that perhaps he wanted to buy a larger house in London but a Highland estate was a hugely different matter.

'Gracious, Edward,' I said. 'That's quite an ambitious plan.'

'Yes, it is,' he confirmed, 'but it fits in with so many of my, or rather our plans, both in the short and long term.' I remained silent as he went on to explain.

'Think of it like this, James. First of all, I want to have some personal input and involvement in the estate and quite frankly, you know as well as I do that it's not going to happen here until I inherit. There's no way that my stepmother is going to let it happen.'

'No, I'm afraid you're right there.'

'Secondly, it gives Elizabeth, myself and our children a country home of our own. Even when we're here at the Folly it still feels like my father has an influence and of course my stepmother's here playing with that bloody tea shop or what-ever she calls it.'

I nodded but didn't comment. It was the old story of trying to work for both sides of a divided family.

Edward continued, 'It's only an hour and a half by plane from London to Inverness and of course a huge attraction for me is the sporting. The estate I'm looking at has an excellent salmon river and deer stalking – two of my greatest passions as you know.'

'Goodness,' I exclaimed, surprised that he had got as far as having a particular estate in mind. 'You're obviously serious if you've looked at somewhere already.'

'Oh, definitely. I've spoken informally to the trustees about the idea and generally they're keen to back it. Basically that's where the money will come from to buy it.'

I reflected on this for a moment. As an idea it did make sense and after all many English landowners had sporting estates in Scotland, so there was nothing unusual in that. It could be a useful way of diversifying the family's assets but Highland estates were notorious for costing more to run than they ever achieved in income. I mentioned this to Edward.

'I appreciate that and you're right,' he said. 'But as a capital asset I think we're safe and I believe that with the right management this particular estate could be marginally profitable.'

'Which estate is it?' I asked, knowing the Highlands quite well.

'It's called Glen Arrin, just west of Inverness,' he explained. 'I've got the sales particulars here,' he added, opening his briefcase to show me.

It was a stunning place. I knew that the photographs would hardly do it justice but even so it took my breath away.

'I don't know that estate,' I said, 'but I know the area. A wonderful part of the Highlands. Well, good luck with it – I think if I was in your position I'd definitely have a go!'

He laughed. 'Well if I get it at least I'll be able to offer you some fishing up there.'

'In that case the official view is that it's an excellent investment,' I joked. 'Let me know if I can help in any way.'

'This is the main reason for coming to see you. I would like you to take a trip there and provide me with a financial appraisal, both capital and expenditure/income wise. See if there's any undeveloped potential or ways of making the sporting better, that sort of thing. I know it's not quite your normal land agency stuff but I've got an agent up there who is willing to help with local and specialist knowledge. I had rather hoped you'd be prepared to oversee it all.'

I paused because this was really outside my duties as deputy agent at Rumshott and although I would love to do it I was employed by his father to run this estate.

As if reading my mind, Edward interrupted my thoughts. 'I've put the idea to my father who would be quite happy for you to spend a couple of weeks sorting it out for me. The only thing is, I haven't mentioned a word of this to George or my stepmother.'

I could imagine why not. Edward didn't get on with either of them and while Lady Leghorn wouldn't mind him disappearing off to Scotland, George would be sure to try to scupper the idea as a rich man's waste of money. Sport to George meant spending money and he only got excited about ideas that generated it.

'Well, I'd love to and thanks for asking me.'

He gave me a file of papers and suggested that I made contact with the present factor, as agents are called in Scotland, to make arrangements to

277

go up and stay.

'Would you mind if Sophie came up with me?' I asked. 'It'd help a lot to have her there as an assistant.'

He laughed. 'An assistant, eh? That's not what I've been hearing!'

'Okay,' I admitted, 'partly assistant and a bigger part pleasure.'

'So it is true then? Can't say I blame you, she's a pretty stunning girl. I could never understand why you didn't do something about it before. Of course take her.'

He stood up. 'Well, thanks for doing this and no doubt we'll speak on the phone next week over the details. Just two other things. Firstly, can you tell George for me, he listens to you better than me! And secondly, when you're in Scotland, and I don't want you to answer this now, try and get a feel of the place and the area to see if perhaps you'd take on the job as factor.'

I must have looked shocked.

'It'd be a promotion from here, after all you're deputy and there you would be in charge, and Elizabeth and I would like it if you wanted the job.'

I was extremely flattered by his confidence in me and so surprised by the offer that I hardly thanked him properly.

After he had left I felt dazed – it all was so unexpected – but I got out the sales details and started to discover what he had in mind to buy. Glen Arrin Estate covered a massive 85,000 acres of some of the most dramatic scenery in Great Britain. It lay approximately forty miles west of

Inverness with mountains that reached over three thousand feet. The Arrin River, which meandered along the central glen, was renowned for its salmon and in addition there was superb trout fishing on some smaller rivers and lochs throughout the estate. The red deer stalking that Edward had mentioned was exceptional and it was evident to see why he was so interested in this estate.

A classic Victorian shooting lodge was situated on the shores of Loch Arrin, white painted with several towers and turrets on each corner. The sale included the estate village, several farms and crofts and a forestry enterprise extending over some 8,000 acres. I couldn't wait to get up there and see it all for myself.

However, the biggest drama was about to happen. I had to break the news to George. I climbed the stairs to his lair and knocked on the door.

'Come in,' he boomed. 'Ah, James. Glad you've come up, take a look at this.'

He passed me a memo from Lord Leghorn.

'Can you deal with it, please. Don't know why he asked me.'

I read the memo.

*To: George Pratt*
*From: Lord Leghorn*
*Re: Butterflies.*
*I read the enclosed article in the Field magazine this month and have since noticed that we have very few butterflies in our gardens. Please arrange for Hawthorne to plant six buddleia trees in appropriate places to rectify the situatio.*

'Yes,' he went on, 'a vital piece of estate management that we somehow overlooked.'

279

'Right, well, whatever his lordship wants,' I confirmed. 'Anyway, I've come up to have a chat with you. Viscount Rumshott's just been in.'

'Yes, I saw his car outside,' he said loudly. 'Something up?'

'You could say that,' I agreed. 'Have you got a few minutes?' and your Ventolin inhaler close at hand I thought to myself.

'Of course I have. Grab a chair.'

I looked around for something to sit on that wasn't already covered in papers, maps or George's sandwiches and ended up dumping some files on the floor.

'There's no point in breaking this to you gently, George, but basically he and Elizabeth have all but bought another estate,' I said and waited for the explosion.

He jumped out of his chair. 'They've done what?' he shouted at me.

'They haven't done anything yet,' I explained, trying to calm him down. 'But their intention is to buy a sporting estate in Scotland.'

'A sporting estate in Scotland,' he cried in disbelief. 'That's the biggest waste of money that any of them have yet come up with. Has he any idea how much those places cost to run?'

'Yes, I think he's...' I started.

'The man's gone completely stark-raving mad. I expect it's some romantic notion of Elizabeth's that's set this off. Go and feed the sweet little doe-eyed deer in the back garden. For crying out loud. Where's the money coming from?'

'George, before you get too incensed...'

'It's too late for that,' he barked. 'I've never

280

heard such rubbish. Why can't he buy an industrial site in Birmingham for instance? He'd get a far better return on his investment.'

He was beginning to wheeze a little and started frantically throwing pieces of paper around searching for his inhaler.

'He wouldn't catch many salmon on an industrial estate in Birmingham, would he?' I replied.

'What's that? Fish? If he wants a fish he can go and buy one at a fishmonger like any normal person, can't he?'

'George, you are deliberately missing the point here and if you just give me a chance I'll explain all he said earlier. There are some factors that even you might approve.'

'The only good thing would be that he wasn't here interfering with this estate. Can't think of any other positive things about it.'

'That's a bit harsh,' I remarked.

'Perhaps it is,' he conceded, 'but what a bloody stupid idea. If he wants to throw money away I can think of easier ways of doing it.'

Once he had calmed down I went through all that Viscount Rumshott had said. It didn't make him any happier about it but he did at least realise that it was out of his hands.

'And he wants me to go up and have a look at it for him. Report back,' I finished.

'No, no, no,' he yelled, pacing about the room. 'We're not getting involved in this. We work for the earl here at Rumshott, not running around some peat bog wasteland in the far north of Scotland.'

'Well I'm afraid I've already agreed to do it. I mean there wasn't much else I could do was there? And apparently he's spoken to his father who has okayed it.'

There was an ominous silence.

'All right but I will make it perfectly clear to all of them that I will have nothing, I repeat nothing, to do with it.'

Well that went pretty well considering, I thought to myself as I walked back to my office.

'What on earth was Mr Pratt shouting about?' asked all the girls waiting with baited breath in the reception hall.

'Lord Rumshott's had an idea that didn't go down very well. I'll tell you about it later. Sophie – have you got a moment, please? I need to talk to you.'

She uncrossed her long elegant legs and stood up to follow me into the calm of my office. The grandfather clock ticked solemnly, its regular beat reminding me that not everywhere was in upheaval.

Our relationship was now quite different to the early days. Sophie wasn't just the pre-college student and nor was the atmosphere tainted with the unease that had coloured our association for so long. We were going out together and it had worked out well. The worries that I had imagined beforehand had never materialised and if anything our office relationship was the better for it. Certainly no one minded. In fact both his lordship and George had approved.

'About bloody time too,' George had said when I told him. 'If you hadn't done something soon I would've thought you had become a pansy!'

I related Viscount Rumshott's conversation to Sophie and told her about the plan that she should come with me to Scotland.

'Only I haven't told George that bit yet so don't say anything to the others. He was a bit jumpy as you gathered without me adding to it.'

'That's fantastic news,' she replied eagerly. 'I adore Scotland. You know Mum and Dad have a place up there, don't you?'

'Yes, I remember you telling me. Somewhere near Oban isn't it?'

'Yeah, an old croft by the sea. It's utterly gorgeous. You'll have to come there one day with me.'

'I'd love to,' I replied, 'but I don't think we'll have time this trip. Edward wants us to go next week by the way. Is that okay with you?'

'Course it is. I know we shouldn't do this but...' and she hugged me, kissing me full on the lips. 'It'll be a bit like going on holiday!'

'A bit, but there'll be a hell of a lot to do. Whatever, it will be fun and it's going to make all the difference being with you.' I hugged her back knowing how lucky I was to have her.

Sophie was right. It was like a holiday and although we spent a great deal of time in the Glen Arrin estate office looking at facts and figures, talking to people and meeting the estate staff, we also had some wonderful days out on the remote stretches of the estate itself.

As I had suspected, the photographs in the sales brochure did not do justice to the landscape. The head stalker, Mr MacPherson, had been in the office the previous day and suggested that we should go and look at a waterfall in the hills behind Glen Arrin Lodge.

'Ye ken tak t'young lassie for a wee hike if ye a mind fer it,' he said with a gleam in his eye. 'An I ken bet ye'll naer find a better spot in t'whole o' t' Highlands!'

We borrowed an estate Land Rover and drove along a rough track that snaked its way into the hills behind the lodge. The countryside became rougher and bleaker the further we went until finally we stopped at a broken bridge. The soft green of the lowlands had given way to steep rock-strewn slopes and yet the massive craggy peaks still soared hundreds of feet above us.

'We've got to walk from here by the look of it,' I said to Sophie.

'Are you ready for it? Mr MacPherson reckoned it was about an hour from here.'

She smiled, her radiant face filling me with a desire to hold her close and never let go.

'Of course I am,' she said. 'I've been looking forward to this since we were told about it.'

We followed a narrow path that ran along the edge of a small rocky burn climbing steeply up the hillside. We were in a little valley hidden by a thick growth of birch and rowan trees stunted by their existence in a barren landscape. We climbed for ages until we finally gained enough height to pass the tree line out on to the open hill. A herd of red deer hinds sprang away in alarm as we rounded a corner of the river and there in front of us, a hundred yards upstream, was the massive waterfall of Moirah burn as it tumbled out of

Loch na Dearg beyond.

We stood together on a rock by the side of the river watching it crashing on the rocks as it fell down the mountain towards the glen floor. The bulk of Celid na Moirah towered behind and the great length of Glen Arrin, bathed in the late afternoon sunshine, spread out in the far distance.

I kissed Sophie, embracing her with a passion so deep and loving that I wondered if I could ever live without her.

'Have you any idea how much I love you, Sophie?' I asked her. 'I've never been so happy in all my life.'

She gazed up at me, her wide honest eyes un-blinking.

'If it's half as much as I love you,' she mur-mured, 'then that's more than I could imagine!'

Everything seemed so perfect just then, so full of promise. We spent two more days exploring the estate. One day we hiked through some of the most breathtaking scenery in the whole of Scot-land before finally staggering on to the peak of Celid na Moirah, over three thousand feet high and stared in wonder across the roof of the High-lands. The Moray Firth was just visible on the east coast and in the other direction the west coast mountains were clearly silhouetted against the blue sky.

On our last night during that first visit to Scot-land we took a boat out fishing on Loch Beinnlaich. The Highlands had cast their spell on us and in the early evening sunshine with the rippling waters of the loch mirroring the great mountains sweeping down to the water's edge the spell became a living dream. Neither of us had ever experienced such magic before and as we let the boat drift slowly along the loch I think we both realised we had discovered something unique. Something that we might never find again.

I sat quietly listening to the lapping of the waves against the wooden hull, the oyster catchers' shrill cries piercing the silence and looked at Sophie. Even the most dramatic setting on earth couldn't diminish her beauty.

'Sophie,' I said, my voice sounding hoarse in the silence, 'if I take this job up here, er, would you come with me?'

She stared back at me, acknowledging what she knew I meant.

'As my wife,' I added.

She leapt towards me rocking the boat alarmingly, her eyes full of happiness.

'Are you firing your assistant then?' she teased.

The publishers hope that this book has given you enjoyable reading. Large Print Books are especially designed to be as easy to see and hold as possible. If you wish a complete list of our books please ask at your local library or write directly to:

**Magna Large Print Books**
Magna House, Long Preston,
Skipton, North Yorkshire.
BD23 4ND

This Large Print Book for the partially sighted, who cannot read normal print, is published under the auspices of

## THE ULVERSCROFT FOUNDATION

## THE ULVERSCROFT FOUNDATION

... we hope that you have enjoyed this Large Print Book. Please think for a moment about those people who have worse eyesight problems than you ... and are unable to even read or enjoy Large Print, without great difficulty.

You can help them by sending a donation, large or small to:

**The Ulverscroft Foundation,
1, The Green, Bradgate Road,
Anstey, Leicestershire, LE7 7FU,
England.**
or request a copy of our brochure for more details.

The Foundation will use all your help to assist those people who are handicapped by various sight problems and need special attention.

Thank you very much for your help.